in columem. Dat in Regia n
Decemb: xvi Ano Dm M° I
arto

bona Soror & Consanguinea

THE BRITISH LIBRARY
HISTORIC LIVES

Queen Elizabeth I

The Charrett Drawne by . 4 . Horses uppo
wth Charrett stood the Coffin Covered wth purple
veluet, & uppo that the representation, The Canapy
borne by 6 Knights.

borne by
Camden
culp Kinge
s.

A Gentleman
usher wth a
white rode.

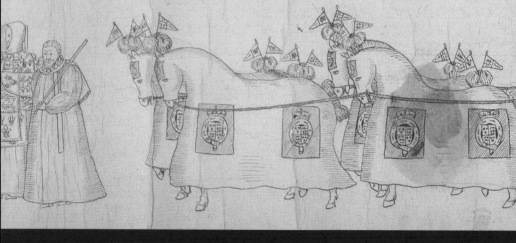

Queen Elizabeth I

Susan Doran

NEW YORK UNIVERSITY PRESS

Washington Square, New York

To Lorraine Harris
with thanks

Cover illustration: Queen Elizabeth I, from the *Guild-book of the Barber-Surgeons of the City of York*. *The British Library, Egerton MS 2572, f11*

Half-title page illustration: Elizabeth in her coronation robes in 1559. *National Portrait Gallery*

Title-page illustration: Elizabeth's funeral procession. *The British Library, MS 5408*

First published in Great Britain in 2003 by
The British Library
96 Euston Road, London NW1 2DB

Designed and typeset by
Andrew Barron @ thextension

Printed in Hong Kong
by South Sea International Press

First published in the U.S.A. in 2003 by
NEW YORK UNIVERSITY PRESS
Washington Square, New York
www.nyupress.org

Library of Congress Cataloging-in-Publication Data
Doran, Susan
Elizabeth I/Susan Doran
p. cm. -(The British Library Historic lives)
Includes bibliographical references and index
ISBN 0-8147-1957-0 (cloth: alk. paper)
1. Elizabeth I, Queen of England, 1533–1603. 2. Great Britain-History-Elizabeth, 1558–1603. 3. Queens-Great Britain-Biography. I. Title. II. Series.

DA357. D67 2003
942.055'092-dc21 2003044931
[B]

The British Library
HISTORIC LIVES SERIES:

Horatio Lord Nelson
Brian Lavery

Queen Elizabeth I
Susan Doran

Contents

Family tree

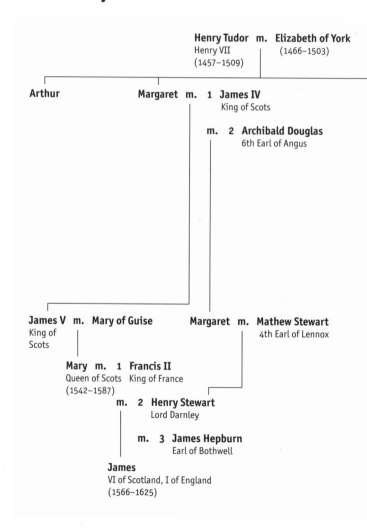

Henry Tudor m. **Elizabeth of York**
Henry VII   (1466–1503)
(1457–1509)

Arthur   **Margaret** m. **1 James IV**
King of Scots

m. **2 Archibald Douglas**
6th Earl of Angus

James V m. **Mary of Guise**   **Margaret** m. **Mathew Stewart**
King of   4th Earl of Lennox
Scots

Mary m. **1 Francis II**
Queen of Scots   King of France
(1542–1587)

m. **2 Henry Stewart**
Lord Darnley

m. **3 James Hepburn**
Earl of Bothwell

James
VI of Scotland, I of England
(1566–1625)

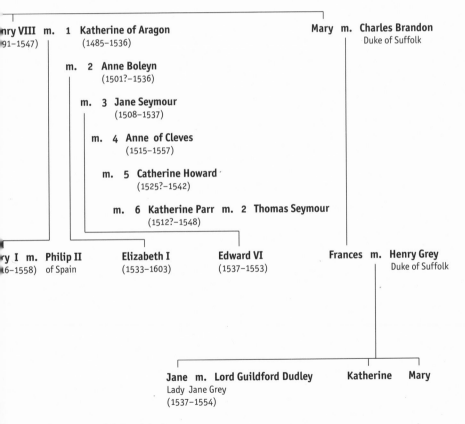

nry VIII m. 1 **Katherine of Aragon**
91–1547)   (1485–1536)

      m. 2 **Anne Boleyn**
           (1501?–1536)

        m. 3 **Jane Seymour**
             (1508–1537)

          m. 4 **Anne of Cleves**
               (1515–1557)

            m. 5 **Catherine Howard**
                 (1525?–1542)

              m. 6 **Katherine Parr** m. 2 **Thomas Seymour**
                   (1512?–1548)

Mary m. Charles Brandon
       Duke of Suffolk

ry I m. **Philip II**   **Elizabeth I**   **Edward VI**   **Frances** m. **Henry Grey**
6–1558) of Spain   (1533–1603)   (1537–1553)   Duke of Suffolk

Jane m. Lord Guildford Dudley   **Katherine**   **Mary**
Lady Jane Grey
(1537–1554)

te: Dates given are those of birth and death

1

But even those people who recognised the legality of the Boleyn marriage struggled with the dates of Elizabeth's conception and birth.

Childhood and adolescence 1533–53

At Greenwich Palace, on Sunday 7 September 1533 between the hours of three and four o'clock in the afternoon, Queen Anne Boleyn gave birth to her first and only child, the future Queen Elizabeth I. King Henry VIII, the new-born baby's father, was immensely relieved at his wife's safe delivery, as he had feared for her life during the labour, and a *Te Deum*, celebrating the birth, was sung in the royal chapel and St Paul's Cathedral in London. Nonetheless, both Anne and Henry were gravely disappointed with the sex of their child, the king's second daughter, for they had both desperately wanted and indeed fully expected it to be a prince, an heir apparent. The celebrations greeting the birth were therefore muted with no bonfires or 'rejoicings', and the jousts planned for the event were immediately cancelled.

The timing of the child's birth, as well as its sex, was unfortunate since it laid Elizabeth open to charges of illegitimacy both during her lifetime and beyond. As far as Roman Catholics were concerned, Elizabeth was unquestionably a bastard, the offspring of an adulterous relationship. In their eyes, Henry's second marriage to Anne was a complete sham because the king was then still married to his first wife Katherine of Aragon. But even those people who recognised the legality of the Boleyn marriage struggled with the dates of Elizabeth's conception and birth. After all, she was born only seven and a half months after her parents' union had been sanctified before a priest (on 24 or 25 January 1533), and less than four months after the annulment of the Aragon marriage had been declared invalid on 23 May 1533. Was she therefore the product of a bigamous or illicit union?

At the time she was born, Henry had no doubts about the legitimacy of his daughter. During the previous six years he had been certain that his earlier marriage to Katherine was invalid, as it had transgressed the laws of affinity in the scriptures which laid down which relatives were forbidden to marry. According

By the Quene

Right trustie and welbiloued we grete you well And wheras it hath pleased the goodnes of
almightie god, of his infinite mercie and grace to sende vnto vs at this tyme good spede in the
delyueraunce and bringing furthe of a prince to the great ioye reioyse and inward comforte of
my lorde vs and of all his good and louing subiectz of this his Realme ffor the whiche his
inestymable benevolence so shewed vnto vs, we haue no litle cause to giue high thankz laude
and praising vnto oure said maker like as we do moost lowly humbly and to all the inward
desire of oure hartz And inasmuche as we vndoubtidly truste, that this oure good spede is to your
great pleasure comforte and consolacion, we therfore by this oure lettr aduertise you therof
desiring and hartely praying you to giue to vs vnto almightie god high thankes glorie
laude and praising, and to pray for the good helth prospitie and continuall preservacion
of the said prince accordingly yeuen vnder oure signet at my lordis Manor of Hampton Court the
xiij day of Septemb. in the xxix yere of my said lordis Reigne

Previous page: The official letter, sent by Queen Anne Boleyn to Lord Cobham, announcing the birth of Elizabeth. Written in advance of Anne's confinement, it is clear that a boy was expected as an 's' had to be squeezed in after the word 'prince' in the third line. *The British Library, Harley MS 283, f.75*

Opposite: Detail of a portrait of Katherine Parr, Elizabeth's last step-mother. The sitter is identified as the Queen by the crown-shaped brooch she wears, which was recorded in her inventory of jewels. *National Portrait Gallery*

to verses Leviticus 18: 16 and 20: 21 of the Hebrew Bible, the marriage of a man to his brother's widow was prohibited and therefore, according to Henry, his own marriage to Katherine was against God's law as she had previously been wed to his elder brother Arthur. In Henry's opinion the pope had only refused to dissolve this marriage, 'cursed by God', because Katherine's nephew, the Emperor Charles V, was exercising military power in the Italian peninsula. Furthermore, as time went by, Henry began to convince himself that the pope had in fact no authority to pronounce on the marriage, and that his annulment case should be heard in England not Rome. In a series of short but significant steps Henry began to deny papal supremacy and to call himself the supreme head of the Church of England, and in 1533 he introduced legislation into the English parliament which made his new title a political reality. The most important of these statutes was the Act of Appeals passed in April, which severed all judicial links between England and Rome. It was immediately followed by the hearing of Henry's matrimonial case at the court of the archbishop of Canterbury in Dunstable, where Archbishop Thomas Cranmer predictably ruled the Aragon marriage to be null and void. By then Anne was pregnant, but this fact did not mean her child was illegitimate. As Henry well knew, according to canon law, a second marriage enacted during annulment proceedings was perfectly valid if the first was eventually terminated. Accordingly on 28 May 1533 Cranmer judged Henry's prior secret marriage to Anne Boleyn to be legal. But when did that marriage take place? A religious ceremony was certainly not held until January 1533; but it is likely that an exchange of vows followed by sexual intercourse – a procedure which in the sixteenth century constituted a valid marriage – had already taken place a couple of months previously. According to the chronicler Edward Hall, Henry 'married privily the Lady Anne Boleyn on Saint Erkenwald's

Day' soon after his return from Calais. Hall's words suggest that on 14 November 1532 (the feast day of the Anglo-Saxon bishop of London, St Erkenwald) a simple ceremony was conducted between Henry and Anne that involved the exchange of vows and sexual consummation. Given Anne's consistent refusal to become Henry's lover before marriage and Henry's obsession with securing a legitimate heir, it seems likely that Hall's dating was accurate and that Elizabeth's conception followed a legal form of marriage undertaken by her parents.

Conspicuously pregnant, Anne was crowned queen at Westminster Abbey, on Whit Sunday, 1 June 1533, in a magnificent ceremony which was designed to silence all doubters. Elizabeth's christening on Wednesday 10 February 1534 provided Henry and Anne with another occasion to announce to the world the legitimacy of their marriage. It was consequently a glittering affair, attended by the leading nobility, members of the royal council, bishops, abbots, and the mayor and aldermen of London. The five-month-old baby wearing a mantle of velvet satin trimmed with ermine was carried in procession under a red canopy in the arms of the premier English noblewoman, the dowager duchess of Norfolk, from Greenwich Palace to the Church of the Observant Friars. Given that the friars had been the most outspoken critics of the Aragon divorce, the choice of venue for the christening was a deliberate gesture of royal defiance and triumph over Anne's enemies. Other supporters of Katherine were also publicly humiliated on the day, as they were forced to participate in the rites of the baptism and to present the baby with expensive gifts after the confirmation. At the same time, Anne's kin and supporters were given prominent roles in the proceedings: her father held the baby's train; her brother helped to carry the canopy; and Archbishop Cranmer was one of three godparents. The baby was named Elizabeth after the grandmother of each of her parents, thus underlining their

Conspicuously pregnant, Anne was crowned queen at Westminster Abbey, on Whit Sunday, 1 June 1533, in a magnificent ceremony which was designed to silence all doubters.

union and her own royal descent. Immediately after the service, she was proclaimed Princess of England and then escorted back to the queen's chamber at Greenwich with a guard of some 500 royal servants carrying lighted torches.

Despite her official status, doubts about Elizabeth's legitimacy continued to be expressed over the next two-and-a-half years, and some questioned whether the young princess would indeed succeed her father if he died without a male heir. Nonetheless, the 1534 Act of Succession confirmed her position as heiress presumptive, and in court and household rituals she was given precedence over Mary, the daughter of Katherine of Aragon, who was bastardised by the same statute. During this period of her infancy Elizabeth seldom saw her parents. Although she had a nursery in her mother's lodgings at Eltham, she was sent out for wet-nursing at Hatfield and her household remained there after she was weaned at twenty-five months. Her parents called at Hatfield for brief and infrequent visits, and she came to court on special occasions. During the Christmas festivities of 1536, when the news of Katherine of Aragon's death reached London, Henry took the child to mass to the fanfare of trumpets 'and other great triumphs' and paraded her before his assembled courtiers 'like one transported with joy'.

All changed, however, in May 1536 when Anne was found guilty of adultery and beheaded at the Tower of London. The execution was immediately followed by the annulment of her marriage to the king, on grounds that were never publicised but probably related to Henry's prior sexual relationship with Anne's sister, Mary Boleyn (which made Anne a form of 'in-law' and therefore within the proscribed degree of affinity). With this legal decision, Elizabeth became a bastard like her half-sister Mary. Soon afterwards, she lost the title of princess and precedence in their joint household, and for a brief period she was even without well-fitting clothes to wear as the king and council no longer paid close attention

The Family of Henry VIII, which was probably commissioned to celebrate the return of Henry's daughters to the succession in 1544. The deceased Jane Seymour and her son, Prince Edward, are depicted with Henry VIII as a close family group, while Mary stands beyond the pillar on the left-hand side and Elizabeth on the right.
The Royal Collection,
© HM Queen Elizabeth II

to her upbringing. Although not yet three at the time, Elizabeth, it was later reported, soon noted the change in her circumstances: 'Why governor,' said she, 'how haps it, yesterday Lady Princess, and today but Lady Elizabeth?'

Given her very limited contact with her mother, it seems improbable that Anne's execution in May 1536 caused Elizabeth deep grief or trauma. Certainly she showed no physical signs of distress and her health remained good until she became troubled with headaches and nephritis during the stressful reigns of her siblings. Nor did Anne's death create an emotional void in her life. She continued with the same nurse or governess, Margaret Lady Bryan, who had been acting as a surrogate mother from the time she was a small baby, and she soon developed a

close relationship with Katherine Champernowne who entered her household probably around 1536. Soon after Lady Bryan left the princess to look after Edward in late 1537, Katherine (whom Elizabeth soon called Kat) took her place and came to act as her governess and intimate companion. In 1545 or 1546 Kat married John Asteley or Ashley, a Boleyn relative by marriage, but she remained Elizabeth's closest servant.

In adult life Elizabeth rarely spoke of her mother, and once queen she made no attempt to clear Anne's name nor declare the validity of her marriage to Henry. Nonetheless, Elizabeth showed respect for her in other ways: she took over both her mother's motto *Semper Eadem* ('Always the same') and her badge of the crowned falcon holding a sceptre perched on a tree stump from which Tudor roses sprang. Later on, she owned a ring (made about 1575) that opened to reveal tiny enamel portraits of herself and her mother. From the outset of her reign, she brought the family of Mary Boleyn, Anne's sister, into her household and service: on her accession she ennobled Mary's son Henry Carey as Lord Hunsdon and gave his daughters important positions in her privy chamber; at the same time she made Sir Francis Knollys, who was married to Mary's daughter Catherine, a privy councillor. Both Knollys and Hunsdon were granted important household posts later in the reign.

The enemies of the Boleyn marriage and Henry's break with Rome took the opportunity of Anne's alleged adultery to claim that Elizabeth was not Henry's daughter at all but instead the child of one of the queen's lovers. Eustace Chapuys, the imperial ambassador, favoured Sir Henry Norris, but others claimed she was the offspring of the musician Mark Smeaton. Roman Catholics in England and abroad repeated the smear both to dishonour Elizabeth and challenge further her right to the throne. Nonetheless, few genuinely believed these accusations, because Elizabeth so clearly resembled the king, particularly in her reddish-gold hair-colouring. Henry VIII had no doubts about her paternity and continued to recognise Elizabeth as his daughter. On rare occasions, he also treated her as an important member of the royal family. At the christening at Hampton Court of her half-brother Edward (the longed-for male heir born to Jane Seymour in October 1537), Elizabeth was given the honour of bearing the chrisom-cloth (baptismal robe), though she was so small that she had to be carried by the prince's maternal uncle in the procession. On the return to the royal apartments she and her half-sister Mary carried the baby's train. In July 1543 they were two of the witnesses at the low-key wedding of her father to his last wife Katherine Parr in the queen's closet next to the royal chapel at Hampton Court. Otherwise though, before 1544, Elizabeth's visits to the royal court were very infrequent and she was usually based in one of the minor royal palaces in the county of Hertfordshire: most often the ex-monastery Ashridge (three miles north of Berkhampstead on the Buckinghamshire border) but also Hatfield, Hunsdon, Hertford Castle and occasionally Enfield.

During the final phase of her father's life, Elizabeth's status changed once again. By early 1544 Henry was preparing to lead his army in a new invasion of France and thought it risky to leave the succession dependent on the life of one child. He therefore decided to restore his two daughters to the succession by parliamentary statute. In the consequent Act of Succession which became law in March 1544 Elizabeth was placed third in line to the throne, after Edward and Mary if they both died without issue, but neither she nor her half-sister was declared legitimate. Furthermore, Henry was empowered to set further conditions concerning the succession either in his will or by letters patent. To commemorate the new settlement of the succession, Henry entertained all his children at a grand dinner and reception in the Palace of Whitehall just before he set off for France, and at about the same time he commissioned a painting, *The Family of Henry VIII*. In the centre of the picture was gathered the intimate family grouping of Henry, the late Queen Jane, and Prince Edward, while Elizabeth and Mary stood in the wings, separated from the central group by pillars. Elizabeth was placed to the left of her father (the least important side) with Mary, a virtual mirror image, on the right.

There is very little available information about Elizabeth's feelings towards her father. The Venetian ambassador commented in 1557 that she 'prides herself on her father and glories in him', and in 1558 the Spanish count of Feria made a similar report. Building on these observations many biographers have written of her deep love and admiration for her father. Admiration she had reason to feel, but her other emotions were undoubtedly more complex. A clue to them may be found in the gifts she presented to both her father and stepmother for New Year's Day in 1545 and 1546. As the exchange of gifts was a formal ritual rather than a true expression of affection, Elizabeth's presents to her family should not be taken at face-value as indicators of the love she bore them, yet the choice and form of these gifts are revealing in other ways. On 31 December 1544, Elizabeth presented Queen Katherine with a hand-written, twenty-seven page translation of a volume of meditations originally composed by Margaret of Navarre, sister of Francis I of France. Every aspect of the work was carefully thought out and resonant in meaning. Its title, the 'Glass of the Sinful Soul' drew attention to Elizabeth's royal lineage since it was a reference to a volume of translations which had been written in 1506 by Margaret Beaufort, her paternal great grandmother, and entitled The Mirror of Gold for the Sinful Soul. The pages were bound within a book cover also made by Elizabeth; on blue cloth she had embroidered a knotwork pattern in silver thread surrounding Katherine's initials, and pansies were sewn in each corner. The 'pansies' both punned with the French word for meditations 'pensées' and, in the language of flowers, sent out the message 'think of me' to Katherine, from whom she had just parted. The embroidered forget-me-nots on the spine of the book signified the 'love' or 'affection' she held for her stepmother. This was a gift then which clearly displayed the eleven-year-old girl's intellectual ability, feminine skills and quick wit, and signalled her duty and devotion to the new queen-consort and by extension the king. It could be seen as a bid to be returned permanently to his affections and a place at court.

But the work may also have expressed a more sinister side to Elizabeth's relationship with her father. One literary scholar, Anne Prescott, has argued that the errors and omissions within Elizabeth's translation reveal at best ambivalent

On 31 December 1544, the eleven-year-old Elizabeth presented her own translation of a French book of meditations, entitled 'Glass of the Sinful Soul', to Queen Katherine Parr as a New Year's gift. The queen's initials 'KP' are embroidered in the centre of the cover and in each corner is a pansy, a pun on the word *pensée* or thought.
Bodleian Library, Oxford

feelings and at worst a strong anger towards her father. Furthermore, the very theme of the meditation – God as a great king and judge who is kind to daughters and merciful to adulterous wives – may be indicative of a deep-rooted, perhaps subconscious, hostility towards that non-merciful king, Henry VIII. If it is true that Elizabeth was working from a copy of the meditations originally owned by Anne Boleyn, as has been postulated, the choice of work is still more suggestive, although Prescott thinks that Elizabeth's translation was based on a later edition published after her mother's execution. Even so, Elizabeth may well have been aware that Margaret of Navarre had been acquainted with Anne during her seven-year stay at the French court and that her mother had owned a copy of the book.

The following New Year's Day, Elizabeth gave gifts of translations to both her father and stepmother, a fact which suggests that the earlier present had been well received. Elizabeth's gift to Katherine on this occasion was an English translation of chapter one of Jean Calvin's *Institution de La Religion Chrestienne*, a choice which drew attention to their common interest in reformed theology. For Henry she translated into Latin, French and Italian a collection of prayers and meditations which Queen Katherine had originally composed in English. The painstaking work of writing out 117 pages in her neatest hand was intended to be seen as a mark of respect towards the king, a compliment to his wife, and of course a testimony to her own industry, intelligence, piety and penmanship. The words of the epistolary preface were calculated to please her father, as they emphasised her duty of obedience to the king and referred to him as 'a god on earth'. At the same time, the gift carefully drew attention to her own royal lineage: in the short preface she referred six times to their familial relationship; and on the elaborately embroidered cover, she included the eglantine rose which

The daughter of Katherine of Aragon could have had little love for the child of Anne Boleyn, the whore (as she saw it) who had supplanted her mother, alienated her from her father, and stripped her of the title of princess.

had been the symbol of her paternal grandmother and namesake, Elizabeth of York. This constant reference to her royal blood-line may be an indication that Elizabeth still did not feel confident of her place in her father's affections and had some anxiety that in the future she might again be ousted from the succession.

Although Henry VIII had married Jane Seymour within weeks of her mother's death, Elizabeth evidently bore no resentment towards her half-brother Edward, and her feelings towards him seem to have been genuinely warm and affectionate. They spent time in each other's company before Edward became king, and their correspondence appears to have been fairly regular when they were apart. On the other hand, Elizabeth's New Year's gifts to her brother – a cambric shirt in 1539 and a needlework 'braser' (to be worn on the arm) – should not necessarily be read as a sign of great sisterly affection because the young princess had taken such trouble to make them herself. As already explained, the presentation of New Year's gifts was a formal ritual, and a child of five or six would have been instructed in what was thought an appropriate token. For his part, from the little we know, Edward also seems to have been very fond of his sister: an informal, loving letter he wrote her on 5 December 1546 reads like a spontaneous outburst of genuine distress at their sudden separation.

Elizabeth's relations with Mary were undoubtedly more problematic. The daughter of Katherine of Aragon could have had little love for the child of Anne Boleyn, the whore (as she saw it) who had supplanted her mother, alienated her from her father, and stripped her of the title of princess. To embitter her further, Mary was forced for over two years to suffer the humiliation of living as the junior member in their joint household. Throughout this time, moreover, her father and Anne put pressure on her to renounce her title, badgering her in the process to defer to the baby she considered the real bastard. Bravely Mary dug in

Opposite: Thomas Seymour, Baron
Seymour of Sudeley, who embroiled
Elizabeth in sexual scandal and
political danger.
National Portrait Gallery

her heels, and 'unless compelled to by sheer force' she resisted serving or playing second fiddle to Elizabeth. Thus, when asked on her arrival at Hatfield in December 1533 if she wished to see the princess, she replied 'that she knew of no Princess in England but herself'. It was not personal spite that inspired Mary to reject her baby sister but loyalty to her mother and concern about her own future; as she well knew, her recognition of the Boleyn child would prejudice her title, rights and marriage prospects.

After the fall of Anne, Mary's treatment at the hands of her father improved and she was immediately given precedence over her younger sister. In these changed circumstances, she could afford to be generous towards the child and in July 1536 she wrote of Elizabeth in glowing terms to their father. As Elizabeth grew up, though, she spent much less time in Mary's company. Now rehabilitated, Mary visited court quite frequently and was allowed to establish her own household at Hunsdon, while Elizabeth was settled for the most part at Ashridge. Only when Queen Katherine brought the royal family together during the summer and early autumn of 1544 did they see each other regularly. Otherwise, the sisters communicated by letter and met formally on state occasions.

It was when Henry departed to fight in the French war in July 1544 that Queen Katherine brought all three of his children to live with her at Hampton Court. During the early autumn she took them on a 'progress' into the counties of Surrey and Kent to escape the plague which had broken out in London. As soon as Henry was known to have returned from France, however, the children were hurriedly sent away. Katherine greeted her victorious husband at Otford in Kent, while Elizabeth and Edward returned to Ashridge. For the remaining two years of Henry's reign, Elizabeth continued to spend most of her time in the country though she made more frequent and sometimes extended visits to court.

Of person rare strong limbs & manly shape
of nature framed to serue on seas & lande
of frindship firm in good state & ill happ
in peace hedde and in ware skill greate bould he
on horse on fete in perill or in pleye
none coulde excell though many did asseye
A subiecte true to Kinge & seruant greate
frind to Gods truth enimye to romes deceu
sumptuose abroad for honnor of the lande
temperate at home yet keepte greate state &
and gaue more mouthes more meate
then some aduanst one higher steps to st
yet agenst nature reason & iust lawes
his blood wase spilt iustles went not cau

At the time of Henry's death (which took place on 28 January 1547) she was staying in her residence at Enfield. She was given the news the next day in the presence of her brother who had been taken there on his way to London from Hertford. She soon followed him to London but, like Mary, she did not attend either her father's funeral or brother's coronation. Again, like Mary, she inherited from her father an income of £3,000 a year until her marriage when she would receive a dowry of £10,000. Henry's will, however, also specified that if either of his daughters married without the consent of the privy councillors he had appointed to rule during Edward's regency, she would lose her place in the succession. Their gender, he clearly believed, made them susceptible to inappropriate romantic attachments while their royal blood made them a prey to ambitious men who did not have the interests of England at heart.

Henry's concern about his daughters' marriages was well founded. No sooner was he dead than the new king's uncle, Lord Thomas Seymour of Sudeley, thought in terms of marrying one of the two daughters of Henry VIII to further his own ambition. Because such a match would never obtain the consent of the council, which was dominated by his elder brother and deadly rival Edward Seymour, duke of Somerset and Lord Protector of the realm, Lord Thomas turned elsewhere and married the Dowager Queen Katherine secretly in mid-April 1547. They only revealed the news of their wedding to Edward VI, the Lord Protector and the council in late June or July.

The thirteen-year-old Elizabeth had gone to live with her stepmother Queen Katherine at her house in Chelsea in April 1547, and soon afterwards Lord Thomas Seymour joined them, sometimes at Chelsea but also at Hanworth in Middlesex or Seymour Place in London. Within a short while, however, gossip began to be circulated that all was not well in the Seymour household. At the very least, Lord Thomas seemed to be showing inappropriate attention to the young princess; at worst he was dabbling in a romantic attachment, making sexual advances, and compromising her reputation. Historians cannot be entirely sure about what really happened but some of the incidents described by Elizabeth's servant, Kat Ashley, read to modern eyes as a form of serious sexual harassment. Evidently Seymour used to come into Elizabeth's room in the mornings and if she were dressed he would 'strike her upon the back or on the buttocks familiarly'. On one occasion he entered her bedchamber in his night-gown; on another he 'strave to have kissed her in her bed' until Ashley 'bade him go away for shame'. So concerned was Ashley that she spoke to Katherine about her husband's behaviour. Though the queen laughed it away, she did promise to accompany him when he came into the princess's bedchamber in the mornings, and thereafter they went to wake her up together and jointly engaged in tickling the young woman in bed. One day in the garden, Seymour scorned at Elizabeth for continuing to wear black in mourning for her father, and he took out his sword and slashed her gown into a hundred pieces while Katherine held her fast. With twenty-first century sensibilities to sexual symbolism this episode seems particularly sinister.

Elizabeth's feelings about her stepfather's attentions are unrecorded. All we know is that she blushed on hearing his name and smiled if he were praised in her presence; but she also began to make sure that she was up and dressed by the time he entered her room. Katherine, however, was growing alarmed. According to a third-hand account, which may be unreliable as it was denied later, she 'came suddenly' upon the two of them when they were alone 'he having her in his arms'. But whatever the provocation, Katherine decided in May 1548 to send Elizabeth away to Cheshunt in Hertfordshire to reside in the household of

Sir Anthony Denny, whose wife was the sister of Kat Ashley. At the point of departure, Katherine delivered a lecture to Elizabeth on the importance of safeguarding her reputation. By Elizabeth's own account, she 'answered little' to this advice, no doubt because she sensed it as a reprimand and was unhappy at her dismissal, but she soon settled at Cheshunt and corresponded with her stepmother in warm and friendly tones. The two never saw each other again. Katherine had been about six months pregnant when Elizabeth had left, and she gave birth on 30 August; five days later she died and the baby survived only a few days longer.

No sooner was Katherine buried than Kat Ashley, who seems to have come under Thomas Seymour's spell, began hinting to Elizabeth that her stepfather was now free to marry her. Seymour had the same idea and began to talk with Sir Thomas Parry, the cofferer or treasurer of Elizabeth's household, and Kat Ashley about a marriage. Though probably attracted to Seymour, Elizabeth prudently did not commit herself. According to Ashley's later account, she answered the question about whether she would marry him if the council agreed with studied vagueness, but she was evidently plagued with anxiety since she started to suffer from severe headaches intermittently after Katherine's death. Meanwhile, Seymour made a failed attempt to gain supreme power by seizing control of the young king and on 17 January 1549 he was sent to the Tower of London. Since rumours of his matrimonial scheme had reached court, Elizabeth's servants, Ashley and Parry, were arrested four days afterwards, while Elizabeth was subjected to interrogation by Sir Robert Tyrwhit at her own house at Hatfield.

Tyrwhit and his wife Elizabeth, who had been trusted members of Katherine Parr's household, had probably heard gossip about Elizabeth and Seymour at Chelsea. Certainly Tyrwhit was convinced that the princess was guilty

Sir Thomas Parry, the treasurer of
Elizabeth's household in Hertfordshire.
A loyal servant in adversity, he was
made a privy councillor on her accession
but died in 1560.
*The Royal Collection, © HM Queen
Elizabeth II*

Thomas Parrie.

of agreeing to marry Seymour against the wishes of the council, conduct which was effectively treason. Elizabeth, however, stood firm in maintaining her innocence: she neither succumbed to the 'good cop, bad cop' tactics of Tyrwhit and Lord Protector Somerset, nor broke down when told of her servants' confessions. She read carefully their depositions and devised a statement which fitted well with their story, namely that she had discussed Seymour with Ashley and Parry but they all agreed she should never marry without the consent of the king and council. 'They all sing one song', complained Tyrwhit, who obviously disbelieved every word of it. Standing on her dignity, appealing to her honour, remaining true to her servants, Elizabeth came through this grim experience with flying colours. Thomas Seymour was executed but Ashley and Parry were released. Elizabeth had begged the Lord Protector to 'be good' to Ashley because of her 'great labour and pain' in bringing her up 'in learning and honesty', and was desperate to take her back into her household. Ashley, however, was only permitted to resume her position in August 1549 and in the meantime Elizabeth was forced to tolerate the presence of Lady Elizabeth Tyrwhit.

Unquestionably Elizabeth's reputation was badly tarnished by the affair, and she had to work hard to rehabilitate herself in the eyes of the king and his council. She wrote affectionate letters to her brother that alluded to their common religious beliefs and rejection of worldly vanities. She devoted herself to her studies and took care to project herself as a serious-minded, pious and obedient princess. She dressed plainly without jewels or gold, and unfashionably left her hair unplaited. While Lord Protector Somerset was in power, she informed him punctiliously of all her doings and would 'know or do nothing which seems important without his understanding'. These tactics served her well, for shortly after her disgrace, Edward VI asked for her portrait presumably to

compensate for her absence from court. Moreover, once Lord Protector Somerset
had fallen from power in October 1549, she was permitted to return to court.
In December of that year she attended the court's Christmas festivities, and other
visits followed until the end of Edward VI's reign. Although by 1550 she had her
own London residence (first Durham Place and then Somerset House) in which
to stay, she was invited on occasion to lodge as the king's guest at St James's
Palace. It was said that in the last years of his life, Edward called Elizabeth his
'sweet sister Temperance'. Princess Mary, by contrast, was out of favour with both
her brother and the new regime because of her continued Catholicism; despite
intense pressure from the king and council, she insisted on hearing mass within
her own household. It was therefore Elizabeth's religion, as much as her subdued
behaviour, that brought her back into favour.

During the second half of Edward's reign Elizabeth became a landowner of
great wealth. Her father's will was settled in 1550 and she could then take formal
possession of manors in Berkshire, Buckinghamshire, Hertfordshire, Lincolnshire,
Oxfordshire and elsewhere. She exchanged some of her lands to acquire Hatfield,
a house that was far more comfortable than the gloomy Ashridge and within easy
access of London. The surveyor of her land, appointed in 1550, was William Cecil,
who was later to become her first principal secretary. Elizabeth's household
comprised some 120 persons and when she rode into London in March 1552
to visit her brother she was accompanied by a retinue of some 200 horsemen.
In the Venetian ambassador's words she had become 'a very great lady'. This was
another reason why the policy-makers at Edward's court could afford to forget
the sexual slander of the past.

Like a number of other 'great ladies' of the Renaissance period, Elizabeth
was given a fine education. Historians know little of the studies she took before

Opposite: Painted about 1546 this is the
earliest surviving portrait of Elizabeth.
Depicted here as a modest and pious
princess, a Bible is open on a lectern beside
her and the book of devotions in her hands
is shown to be used, as her place is marked
with her finger and bookmark.
The Royal Collection, © HM Queen Elizabeth II

the end of her tenth year but it seems likely that she initially learned her lessons
with Kat Ashley and received occasional tuition in the classics from her brother's
tutors. In 1544, however, Elizabeth was allowed her own private tutor, the
Cambridge humanist scholar, William Grindal, and under his care she blossomed
intellectually so that by the time he unexpectedly died of the plague in January
1548 she was fluent in Italian, French and Latin and had some knowledge of
Greek. On his death, her step-parents wanted Francis Goldsmith (Queen
Katherine's chaplain) to be his replacement but Elizabeth, who had both admired
and grown fond of Grindal, insisted on the appointment of his one-time teacher
and friend, Roger Ascham, who was then a fellow of St John's College
Cambridge. It was a mark of her strong personality that she got her own way.

Ascham stayed with Elizabeth for nearly two years and described her
studies to his friend the Protestant theologian Jacob Sturmius. Every morning
she studied Greek with him, beginning with a passage from the Greek New
Testament and moving on to literary writers such as Sophocles and rhetoricians
like Isocrates. In the afternoon she worked on Latin authors and in the evenings
they read together one of the two classical models of style, the orator Cicero
and the historian Livy. Ascham supplemented her religious instruction with
the writings of the third-century bishop St Cyprian, who had emphasised the
importance of the unity of the Church, and with *The Commonplaces*, a work of
the contemporary Lutheran theologian Philip Melancthon; both these writers,
Ascham believed, conveyed 'pure doctrine in elegant language'.

Ascham's method of study was 'double translation', a rigorous linguistic
training whereby his pupil translated a passage into written English and then
back into its original language, attempting to reproduce its precise words. The
purpose, explained Ascham, was not only to teach grammar and vocabulary but

also the style and mindset of the original authors. Finally Ascham taught Elizabeth penmanship, the newly fashionable Italian (italic) script which served her well until old age. Elizabeth thrived under this rigorous regime, and it bred in her a love of classical learning which did not end with the period of instruction. Once queen, she brought Ascham into royal service as her Latin clerk and read Greek with him until he died. Her classical education helped her perform her duties as queen, for she spoke Latin in public arenas, delivering orations to the universities and giving speeches to foreign ambassadors.

In addition to the classics and religion, Elizabeth learned modern languages. Native speakers in her household provided expert tuition and practice in conversation: Giovanni Battista Castiglioni taught her Italian as well as the lute; Blanche Parry, a lady-in-waiting, was probably responsible for teaching her to speak Welsh. Elizabeth showed considerable confidence in speaking foreign languages and her fluency was probably better than her accuracy. At any rate, Ascham noted that as a young teenager she spoke Greek 'frequently, willingly' but only 'moderately well'. Her spoken French was said to be excellent but, judging from her personal letters in the 1580s to the duke of Anjou, her competence in written French was considerably less proficient, marred by poor grammar and unidiomatic expression, though it is possible that she had forgotten grammatical rules over time. Despite her academic education, the skills expected of an aristocratic woman were not neglected, and Elizabeth was taught to be an accomplished dancer, archer, rider, needle-woman and musician, playing the lute and virginal (an early form of spinet).

Because of all these accomplishments Elizabeth is often viewed as some kind of genius. She was certainly a talented and motivated learner, but she was far from unique in her quick wit, scholarship and abilities. Numerous other aristocratic women of the Tudor period who had been exposed to a humanist education (including Margaret More and her daughter Mary Roper, Lady Jane Grey, the sisters Mildred and Anne Cooke, and Mary Sidney countess of Pembroke) displayed a similar intelligence, facility with languages and knowledge of classical authors. They all possessed the discipline, intellect and leisure to benefit from the careful tutoring and wide-ranging curriculum which had previously been offered only to men.

The men and women responsible for Elizabeth's intellectual and spiritual education during both her father and brother's reign favoured religious reform. Through them, Elizabeth was exposed from an early age to writers who questioned or even rejected orthodox Catholic teachings about purgatory, the miraculous power of saints, and the role of 'works' in salvation, and emphasised the importance of the scriptures as the source of Christian knowledge and model for godly behaviour. For good reasons, historians prefer to call these religious ideas 'evangelical' rather than Protestant, but it easy to see how believers in them could move on to take up Protestant positions on key doctrinal issues: the assertion of justification by faith alone; the denial of the priest's sacerdotal power; the rejection of transubstantiation, and the dismissal of the doctrine that the mass was a re-enactment of Christ's sacrifice and instrument for individual redemption. Elizabeth appears to have taken the important steps towards Protestantism during Edward VI's reign. No doubt the influence of Katherine Parr, her tutor Roger Ascham, and new Protestant chaplain, Edmund Allen, as well as Sir Anthony Denny and his wife, in whose house she stayed during part of 1548, all played their part in this process, and by 1551, when she had reached eighteen years of age, the imperial ambassador noted that she 'has embraced the new religion'.

2

From the very beginning of Mary's
reign in 1553, it was obvious that the
two sisters would clash over religion.

The challenge of Mary I's reign 1553–58

In the spring of 1553 Edward VI fell seriously ill with consumption. Close to death in June, he made arrangements to remove both his half-sisters from the line of succession. His desire to exclude Mary is understandable, as he rightly feared that she would undo all his Protestant reforms, but his reasons for excluding Elizabeth are less obvious. Perhaps he could not find logical grounds to exclude the one daughter of Henry VIII without the other; maybe he thought Elizabeth would not agree to be advanced before her sister. Possibly too, he was concerned that Elizabeth might marry a Catholic in the future and thus also endanger the recently established Protestant settlement. Whatever the case, Edward left the throne to his cousin, Lady Jane Grey, who was married to the son of his chief adviser, John Dudley duke of Northumberland. When Edward died on 6 July 1553, his council proclaimed Jane queen, but Mary immediately challenged her title and succeeded in toppling the usurper without a fight on a wave of popular support.

Publicly, at least, Elizabeth bore no bitterness against her brother for disinheriting her in July 1553, and she may well have blamed Northumberland, rather than Edward, for the attempt to overturn Henry VIII's will and the 1544 Act of Succession. At any rate, once Mary had seized the throne, Elizabeth made a strong statement of her continuing loving feelings towards her brother by wearing at her waist a gold miniature book, two inches square, which contained the prayer which the young king had supposedly made three hours before his death.

From the very beginning of Mary's reign in 1553, it was obvious that the two sisters would clash over religion. Elizabeth absented herself from the requiem mass that Mary had ordered for their dead brother, and excused herself from services in the royal chapel. When it became clear that this conduct was offending

Previous page: Elizabeth's half-sister Mary, who became queen of England in 1553. A staunch Catholic and loyal daughter of Katherine of Aragon, she made Elizabeth's life very difficult during her reign.
National Portrait Gallery

the queen and her council, Elizabeth requested a private audience with her sister to explain her position: she had, she said, been educated according to the Protestant religion and 'had never even heard the doctrines of the old faith'. She then entreated the queen to provide her with learned instructors and Catholic books to see if 'the reading would enable her to overcome her scruples'. A few days afterwards, on 8 September 1553, she attended mass for the first time but made a public display of her reluctance to go, complaining loudly 'all the way to church that her stomach ached, wearing a suffering air'. It was no wonder that an observer commented: 'everyone believes she is acting rather from fear of danger and peril than from real devotion'. For a time Mary was prepared to believe that her sister was sincere and would eventually embrace the 'true religion'. She therefore rewarded Elizabeth's 'conversion' with a present of a rosary made from white coral, and behaved towards her with conspicuous honour and affection by, for instance, seating the princess by her side during dinner and supper. At Mary's coronation, Elizabeth was given pride of place as heiress to the throne: in the procession to the Tower on the evening before the event she sat in the first chariot with her surviving stepmother Anne of Cleves, 'both dressed in silver after the French fashion'; at the coronation, she carried the queen's train; and at the post-coronation banquet she sat at the central table on one side of the newly crowned queen.

Once the coronation was over, however, everything changed. One of Mary's first actions was to enact a parliamentary statute that effectively reinforced Elizabeth's bastardy, since it declared the legality of the marriage between Henry VIII and Katherine of Aragon. After this, wrote the Venetian ambassador, 'a great change took place in Queen Mary's treatment of her [Elizabeth] ... she now by all her actions shows that she held her in small account'. At the same time the queen lost patience with Elizabeth for only intermittently attending Catholic services. In November Mary confided to her minister, Lord Paget, and the imperial ambassador that she would like to exclude her sister from the succession because she was a heretic and a bastard. Later that month, after a banquet at court, she ordered Elizabeth to yield precedence to Frances, duchess of Suffolk (whose daughter Lady Jane Grey was in prison for treason) and Lady Margaret Douglas, countess of Lennox, both of whom were daughters of Henry VIII's two sisters. Nor was this an isolated snub, for Elizabeth was compelled on other occasions to give her cousins precedence. By December, the situation had become intolerable and she requested permission to leave court for her home in Hertfordshire. Mary agreed and the sisters parted amicably, or at least outwardly so. Mary presented Elizabeth with a gift of a sable stole while the latter still held out the possibility of a conversion. She even asked Mary to send her vestments, chalices and other Catholic ornaments so that masses could be heard in her household.

In reality, as Mary had correctly surmised, Elizabeth and her household were firmly Protestant. In offering to conform Elizabeth had no intention of giving up her faith, but was adopting a stance known as Nicodemism. In the Bible, Nicodemus had visited Christ only by night as he had feared for his life, and many Protestants during Mary's reign – including Elizabeth's ex-tutor Ascham and future minister William Cecil – decided to follow the scriptural precedent, in other words to conform outwardly and await better times. Otherwise they would be at risk of prosecution under the heresy laws, and in danger of being burned at the stake. Out of public view at Ashridge or Hatfield, Elizabeth kept Protestants about her, read from English Bibles, and prayed in English.

Shortly after Elizabeth's departure from court, a rebellion erupted against Mary's rule, which put the princess in serious danger. Mary's determination to

A contemporary map of London,
which shows the Tower north of the
river to the right.
The British Library, Sloane MS 2956, f.52*

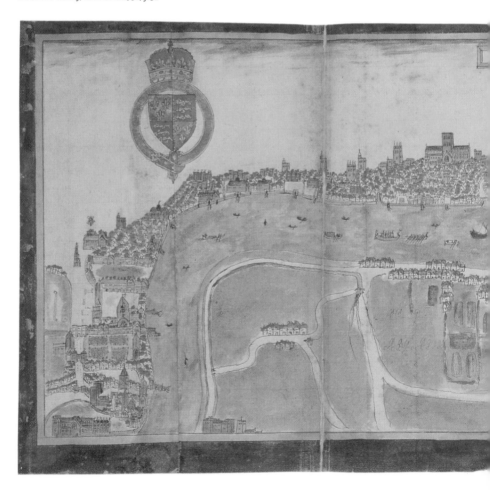

marry her cousin, Philip of Spain, the son of Charles V, had so dismayed some English courtiers that they conspired to marry Elizabeth to Edward Courtenay, earl of Devon, an Englishman of Yorkist descent, and place them both on the throne. Originally, the conspirators had planned four co-ordinated risings – in the Welsh borders, South, South-West, and Midlands – but only the county of Kent actually came out in rebellion. In late January 1554, a force of 3,000 men under the leadership of Sir Thomas Wyatt marched to London, where they were repulsed. On 7 February, Wyatt was captured and brought to the Tower.

Even before Elizabeth had left for Hertfordshire, suspicions had been aired at court that she was conspiring against Mary with the French ambassador who was trying to stop the Spanish marriage. Consequently, no sooner had the rebellion broken out than Mary decided to play safe and place Elizabeth securely in custody. On 26 January 1554 she informed the princess by letter of the rising and summoned her back to court for her own protection. Well aware of the danger, Elizabeth pleaded illness and declined to leave her home, but four days after Wyatt's submission, on 11 February, three of Mary's councillors accompanied by 250 horsemen arrived at Ashridge with instructions to escort Elizabeth to court. By this time, if not before, Elizabeth was genuinely sick with nephritis, a condition brought on by nervous strain, and she begged to be allowed to remain at Ashridge until she recovered, but the queen's physicians pronounced that she could travel with no hazard to her life. The following day, leaving Kat Ashley behind, she began a slow journey to London, being led 'more like a prisoner than a prince'. In the early hours of the morning of 23 February she arrived at Westminster in an open carriage so that anyone who was about could see that she was sick, her face pale and swollen. Dressed in white, she intended to look the picture of innocence.

> 'I pray to God', she wrote, 'that...
> evil persuasions persuade not one
> sister against the other'. When she
> came to the end of the letter... she
> carefully scored across the remainder
> of the page to prevent her enemies
> from inserting a forged confession.

For three weeks Elizabeth was left isolated in Whitehall Palace, while the council interrogated the conspirators. They had so far found three strong but circumstantial pieces of evidence against her and hoped to uncover more. The first concerned messages she had received from Wyatt and another leading conspirator, advising her to move to her castle at Donnington in Berkshire. The second was a copy of a letter from her, discovered amongst the dispatches seized from a courier of the French ambassador. From this it was concluded that she had been in regular communication with the French who were thought to be implicated in the rebellion. The third related to the fact that a gentleman in her service, Sir William St Loe, had been seen with the rebels. The government, however, possessed no evidence that she had had any communication with Courtenay, had written to the conspirators, or indeed knew about the rebellion. If, as seems likely, she had been in contact with the conspirators, she covered her tracks well.

On 15 March Elizabeth was examined by members of the council headed by Stephen Gardiner, bishop of Winchester and lord chancellor. Throughout the interrogation, she denied any knowledge of or involvement in the plot, but she was not believed and the next day the marquis of Winchester and earl of Sussex arrived to accompany her to the Tower. Terrified that she would be summarily condemned and executed, Elizabeth decided her only hope lay in appealing to her sister in person. She therefore entreated her noble guards to let her write to Mary with a request for an audience. Reluctantly they succumbed to her pleas, and Elizabeth set to work to produce a carefully composed letter that would play upon Mary's 'natural kindness' and sisterly feelings: 'I pray to God', she wrote, 'that ... evil persuasions persuade not one sister against the other'. When she came to the end of the letter, she had only filled a quarter of the second sheet, and she carefully scored across the remainder of the page to prevent her enemies from inserting a forged confession. Mary, however, was unmoved by her sister's desperate petition and refused to see her. The next day, the morning of Palm Sunday, Elizabeth was conveyed to the Tower by barge and in the rain. She was accompanied by three gentlewomen (but not Kat Ashley who had remained behind at Ashridge for interrogation), her gentleman usher and two grooms of her chamber. The water-way was empty as most of the citizens of London would have then been at church.

Contrary to popular belief, the princess did not land at Traitors' Gate; instead, because it was low tide, she disembarked 'at the drawbridge'. True to form, she did not enter the Tower as a demoralised prisoner but on the contrary made a powerful protest against her wrongful arrest. According to the martyrologist John Foxe's account of 1563, she sat down in the rain on the steps of the landing stage, refusing to enter the precinct, and only after one of her gentlemen ushers broke down in sobs would she march in. Although some of her escorts and guards were clearly uneasy at imprisoning the heiress presumptive, others treated her without compassion, or indeed consideration of their own futures when she might be queen. Sir John Gage, the constable of the Tower, locked the doors 'very straightly' behind her in a room on the first floor of the Bell Tower and placed a strong guard at the door. When her servants complained that the room contained only three small windows, he threatened to throw them 'where they could neither see sun or moon'.

On 11 April 1554 Wyatt was executed. On the scaffold he exonerated Elizabeth: 'I take it upon my death that they [Elizabeth and Courtenay] never knew of the conspiracy', but the following day members of Mary's council interrogated Elizabeth hoping to squeeze a confession out of her. She gave

nothing away. By mid-April, she was allowed a little more freedom and permitted to walk in a private garden. Mary, however, still distrusted her and even suspected that the son of the keeper of the wardrobe, a child of about four years of age, was passing on secret messages when he regularly gave her nosegays of flowers during her walks. As a result, the walks were discontinued. Throughout this time, Mary was evidently hoping to build a stronger case against Elizabeth so that she could be put on trial and found guilty. Mary also listened to the imperial ambassador who was advising her to order Elizabeth's execution, even without conclusive proof of guilt. But Elizabeth was protected by a group of Mary's councillors, including Lord William Howard of Effingham and Henry, earl of Sussex, who were both kinsmen through Anne Boleyn. Apart from family feeling, these men were motivated by concerns about the succession. They feared that if Elizabeth were executed, the succession would be open and uncertain until Mary had a child; and, if Mary proved barren, England might well slip into a civil war over the succession on her death.

Eventually, Mary had to accept that no proof could be found to implicate Elizabeth in the rebellion, but she still thought it unsafe to release her. She therefore decided to put the princess under house-arrest at the royal hunting lodge at Woodstock in Oxfordshire, some distance from London, at least until her marriage to Philip was solemnised and an heir was born. On Trinity Sunday 19 May an armed guard took the twenty-year-old Elizabeth by barge to Richmond Palace from where she travelled to Woodstock, making three overnight stops on the way: at West Wycombe, Windsor and Rycote. Throughout the journey, men and women flocked to see her; at Rycote housewives plied her with cake and wafers when she passed; and at Aston, the church bells were rung to celebrate her freedom. But Woodstock was no place of freedom. Elizabeth was kept under constant guard by Sir Henry Bedingfield, her gaoler. He permitted her neither visitors nor messages and referred all her requests back to the council for approval.

Elizabeth's most persistent request during her imprisonment was for an English Bible. Though not illegal, her demand revealed her continuing commitment to the religion of her youth, for it was well known that she could read Latin as easily as English. Although Elizabeth attended the Latin mass alongside Bedingfield, her household at Woodstock was as evangelical as she could make it without breaking the law. She made sure the litany was performed in English, and heard it two or three times a week. When challenged, she submitted but protested that an English litany had been 'set forth in the King my Father his days' and that the litany (prayers of supplication) was appropriate for someone wrongfully imprisoned. Furthermore at least four of her six servants refused to conform and attend mass, while the rest did so 'for form only'. Nicodemite though she was, Elizabeth took risks to keep true to her conscience.

Despite the close watch on her, Elizabeth did have contact with the outside world. Parry, her cofferer, took residence in the Bull Inn at Woodstock, ostensibly in order to manage her financial affairs but also to keep in communication with his mistress. Other friends and supporters congregated at the inn, intent on passing on or receiving messages. Furthermore, as Elizabeth often won the battle of wills between herself and Bedingfield, she was eventually sent her Bible, given leave to write letters to the queen and council, and allowed to see the royal physicians instead of those initially offered. Nonetheless, it suited Elizabeth later in life to present her time at Woodstock as one of great discomfort and danger. Foreign visitors visited the hunting lodge almost as a place of pilgrimage during her reign. There, they were shown verses she had scratched on a window pane and were told about the horrors of Elizabeth's days as a prisoner when she was allowed no paper, pen or ink, had feared for her life and said she envied the milkmaid.

At last in April 1555, Bedingfield was ordered to bring Elizabeth to Hampton Court. This move was probably the idea of Philip of Spain, who had married Mary in July 1554 and now believed that his wife was in the last stages of pregnancy (erroneously as it turned out). He wanted Elizabeth at court in case Mary died in childbirth. Elizabeth's presence there, he reasoned, would ensure her succession and prevent that of Mary Stewart, the thirteen-year-old queen of Scotland. As the granddaughter of Margaret, the elder sister of Henry VIII, Mary Stewart had a strong claim to the succession; since she was betrothed to the dauphin (heir to the French throne), that claim was backed by the king of France, who was the traditional and present enemy of Spain.

Elizabeth remained in isolation at Hampton Court for two weeks and, as one seventeenth-century historian wrote, 'she seemed to have changed the place but not the prison'. At last, unexpectedly, at ten o'clock at night, she was brought

Opposite: These seventeenth-century pictures depict Elizabeth's trials during Mary's reign. The first shows a child offering a nosegay to Elizabeth during one of her walks in the precincts of the Tower. The second portrays Elizabeth's interview with Queen Mary at Hampton Court in May 1555. Peeping through the curtain is King Philip.
Bridgeman Art Library

to see the queen. The year in prison had not broken her spirit and she refused to admit to any offence, despite Mary's chilly reception and demand that she submit. The sisters consequently parted without any evident reconciliation, yet a week later Bedingfield and his guard were dismissed. Elizabeth was to be allowed to remain at Hampton Court, still under a light guard but with her own household. It was Philip who was probably responsible for Elizabeth's release and gradual return to court life. By now he realised that Mary's pregnancy was a delusion, and that indeed she might never conceive an heir. In these circumstances it was in Spanish interests for Elizabeth to be returned to favour and be found a Catholic husband who was an ally of his family. By this means he could keep England within Spain's sphere of influence. All he needed was to get his wife and sister-in-law to agree in principle to a marriage and accept his choice of candidate.

During the reigns of both Henry VIII and Edward VI, there had been some attempts to arrange a marriage between Elizabeth and a son of one of the European kings. The negotiations, however, had consistently come to nothing mainly because of the girl's legal status as a bastard, which was considered dishonourable and thought likely to prejudice her claim to the English throne. There had also been a suggestion early in Mary's reign that Elizabeth might marry Courtenay but the queen rejected any such idea as potentially too dangerous. In 1555 Philip chose Prince Emmanuel Philibert of Piedmont who was the titular duke of Savoy as the best candidate for the hand of Elizabeth: he was Catholic, an ally of Spain, of royal blood, and the right age. At that time, though, Philip was preoccupied with his plans to leave England while the duke was more concerned with recovering his lands from the French.

Elizabeth had obtained permission to leave court and travel to Hatfield in

The L. Elizabeth *Prifoner in the Tower*

The L. *Elizabeth before her Sifter Q. Mary*

October 1555. There she was reunited with Kat Ashley and resumed her studies under Ascham who returned to her service after a five-year break. Despite the seeming innocence of the princess's occupations, her household became first the centre of a plot against the queen and thereafter the court of a queen-in-waiting. The plot against Mary is usually known as the Dudley conspiracy, named after Sir Henry Dudley, one of its leading conspirators. Like the earlier Wyatt's rebellion, the 1556 plot aimed to put Elizabeth on the throne but it foundered before any armed rising occurred. When the government started sniffing out suspects, they alighted on members of Elizabeth's household and arrested five servants including Francis Verney, Kat Ashley and Giovanni Battista Castiglione. Verney was so deeply implicated in the plot that he was put on trial and found guilty of treason (though pardoned), while Ashley and Castiglione denied complicity but were sent briefly to the Tower and removed permanently from their mistress's household.

Anti-Catholic books and seditious papers had been discovered in a cabinet said to belong to Ashley, while Castiglione had already been under suspicion for disseminating subversive literature in London.

Very likely Elizabeth was not as ignorant about the activities of her household servants as she was to claim, and her protestations of innocence no doubt sounded hollow to Mary. Nonetheless, she was not arrested nor even placed under an armed guard; instead, the privy councillor, Sir Thomas Pope, was sent to Hatfield in June to keep an eye on her, but he was instructed to treat her honourably as suited her status. Four months later he was discharged and Elizabeth was invited to court. This mild treatment contrasted strongly with the lengthy interrogations, imprisonment and custody Elizabeth had endured after Wyatt's rebellion, but the reason is not hard to find. In mid-1556 few people believed that the queen would produce an heir, and consequently both her English councillors and Spanish husband wanted Elizabeth kept alive and at liberty to prevent a later disputed succession that might well end in a civil war or a French invasion to put Mary Stewart on the throne.

In these circumstances, a Catholic marriage for Elizabeth seemed to be urgently required. In December 1556, therefore, Philip returned to the Savoy project and put it to his wife. Mary had invited Elizabeth to court for Christmas, and it seems likely that the queen raised the question of the match shortly after Elizabeth's arrival on 28 November. Elizabeth's reply can only be guessed at; all we know is that she returned to Hatfield on 3 December well before Christmas. Pressure on Elizabeth to marry Savoy was resumed when Philip returned to England again in April 1557. This time both Mary and Elizabeth proved intractably opposed to the scheme. Mary refused to acknowledge Elizabeth's legitimacy and status as heir, which was a necessary prerequisite of the match.

Elizabeth objected because she would completely lose her freedom of action; the marriage would commit her to a religion she fundamentally opposed and, once she became queen, to a pro-Spanish foreign policy. Neither sister would budge.

Another matrimonial proposal was presented to Elizabeth in November 1557, this time from an utterly unexpected quarter. The king of Sweden sent an envoy to England to seek Elizabeth's hand for his son Eric. Ignorant of court protocol, the envoy went directly to the princess instead of to the queen, an action that aroused all Mary's latent suspicions about her sister. She immediately dispatched Sir Thomas Pope to Hatfield to make inquiries, but Elizabeth satisfied him that she had never had any previous communication with the Swedes and had no intention of marrying the prince, or (then at least) anyone else.

Based at Hatfield during the last years of Mary's reign, Elizabeth only paid occasional and short visits to London. She then rode in with a 'great company' of men to display her power as a major landowner and heir to the throne. Her household, at this time, was noticeably increasing. Because Mary was in poor health and not expected to live long, 'there is not a lord or gentleman in the kingdom', wrote the Venetian ambassador, who did not endeavour 'to enter her [Elizabeth's] service himself or to place one of his sons or brothers in it'. For her part, Elizabeth had good reason to employ these men: there was a strong possibility that she would have to fight for the throne against a Catholic contender. At the same time Elizabeth was in regular communication with members of Mary's court and council who kept her abreast of political events and debates.

In October 1558 it was evident that Mary was dying. Elizabeth consequently stepped up her preparations for securing her inheritance. She brought into her orbit key political and military figures who, she hoped, could deliver the kingdom to her, and she used the home of Sir John Brocket, two-and-a-half miles north of Hatfield, as a base for directing operations. By this time, Mary had reluctantly accepted the inevitable – that her sister would be the next queen – but she still wanted reassurance that Elizabeth would make no changes to religion. She therefore sent her gentlewoman, Lady Jane Dormer, to Hatfield in early November with instructions that she should relinquish her jewels to Elizabeth in return for a promise that once queen she would maintain the Catholic faith. According to Dormer, Elizabeth took the jewels and swore that she was a true Roman Catholic. If this account is true, Elizabeth proved to be considerably more honest when she spoke several days afterwards to an envoy from Philip. The count of Feria was trying to persuade Elizabeth that she owed her throne to Philip so that she would feel dependent on him and follow policies in the Spanish interest, but Elizabeth's statements made him very pessimistic about the future. Elizabeth, he told Philip, believed she owed her throne not to him but to 'the attachment of the people of England', and she would therefore prove independent of Spain. Most worrying of all, from his point of view, she would 'not be well-disposed in matters of religion' and would rule with the help of her Protestant friends.

Between five and six in the morning of Thursday 17 November 1558 Mary died. Around noon Nicholas Heath, archbishop of York and lord chancellor, proclaimed Elizabeth's accession in the parliament which was then in session, and soon afterwards proclamations were read out at Whitehall and elsewhere in London. According to a London chronicler the news was immediately greeted with bell-ringing, and later that evening with bonfires and merry-making. Even if Mary had been immensely popular, Londoners would have taken advantage of a street party but during the last year of her reign Mary was far from liked. Her

illness and deluded belief – for a second time – that she was pregnant was turning her into a laughing stock as well as paralysing the government. To make matters worse, famine and epidemics were mowing down the population at an alarming rate, while prices had soared and the currency was corrupt after years of debasements under Henry and Edward. As a final blow, war against France had ended with the humiliating loss in January 1558 of Calais, a territory which had been in English hands since 1347. Given these failures, the accession of a new monarch was a cause of celebration for all but the most committed Roman Catholic subjects. Certainly there was no guarantee that a twenty-five-year-old, inexperienced woman might do better, but in November 1558 it probably seemed to many that she could hardly do any worse!

As for Elizabeth herself, she had grown in stature during the last years of Mary's reign, and she was fit and ready to take on the heavy responsibilities of governing a realm divided over religion and demoralised by military defeat.

3

Establishing the regime 1558–65

Elizabeth heard the news of her sister's death when a messenger arrived to bring her Mary's black enamelled ring which had been a betrothal gift from Philip. Well prepared for this event, Elizabeth started immediately on the work of government. She had already determined some weeks earlier that her principal secretary would be Sir William Cecil, a kinsman of Sir Thomas Parry and a man whom she had known for at least ten years. Cecil had studied Greek and Latin at Ascham's college in Cambridge and shared the outlook of a group of lay humanists who were immersed in the classics and committed to public service. Like them he was also a committed Protestant, and like Elizabeth he was a Nicodemite outwardly conforming under Mary. Most important of all he had acted as secretary to Lord Protector Somerset and as principal secretary under Northumberland and was thus experienced in government. He began work on the first day of Elizabeth's reign although he was not formally appointed until three days afterwards, when the queen held her first council meeting.

Elizabeth began appointing the rest of her council at Hatfield, where she spent the first five days of her reign. She then journeyed to London but only entered the City on 28 November. The earl of Pembroke led the procession to the Tower, bearing the upright sword of state, and she followed on horseback, dressed in purple velvet, the colour of royalty and imperial power. She wore a scarf about her neck, because it was a chilly day. Despite the cold, the Londoners turned out in force to see her, and in a style that was to become her distinctive characteristic, Elizabeth played to the crowd: 'her eye was set upon one, her ear listened to another, her judgement ran upon a third, to a fourth she addressed her speech'. For the next five days she stayed in the Tower, moving on St Nicholas's Eve into Somerset House on the Strand where she resided until Mary's funeral and burial were over.

The pencioners wth out head on fote wt pollaxes in ther handes bareheded

The Quiers and stemen next about her highnes litter bareheded

The Lorde Chamberlayn / the ... ... berehed

The palfrey of honour

Bearinge the canapye on eche syde g knyghtes

Bearing g ye mayster the L Stiles pamlet

Bearinge the forsse worth the L Chamb'lain Dudley

The Quiers and stemen next about her highnes litter bareheded

The pencioners wth out head on fote wt pollaxes in ther handes bare hedd

Previous page: This drawing of the coronation procession on 14 January 1559 shows Elizabeth in a canopied litter led by white horses. On each side of her are rows of figures, who include the gentlemen of the privy chamber and her gentleman pensioners. Heading the procession behind her is Robert Dudley, master of the horse.
The British Library, Egerton MS 3320, f.4v-5

Opposite: Elizabeth in the robes she wore for her coronation service in 1559. The sleeves and bodice were newly made to fit Elizabeth, but the garments had also been used by Mary on her coronation day. The gold cloak was lined with ermine and the gold crown set with diamonds, rubies, sapphires, and pearls.
National Portrait Gallery

Elizabeth moved into Whitehall Palace for the Christmas festivities, which were noted as being lively despite the period of mourning, but work was not forgotten. The coronation was due to take place on 15 January, the date thought propitious by the astrologer Dr John Dee, and thought was given during Christmas week to the content and style of the pre-coronation ceremonies as well as to the sensitive issue of what form the religious service should take. Traditionally on the afternoon before the coronation the monarch would progress through the City from the Tower towards Westminster, and along the route he or she would be greeted by pageants and recitations devised and performed by Londoners. The pageants of 1559 were political in theme, focusing on Elizabeth's right to the throne, the virtues of good government (which included 'pure religion' or Protestantism), the triumph of Time, (meaning Protestantism), and the biblical example of Deborah (the female judge who had successfully destroyed idolatry). Taken together the pageants implicitly represented a refutation of the view recently expressed by the Scottish Calvinist John Knox that women had no right to rule, and explicitly coupled the queen 'with the Gospel and verity of God's holy word', in other words the Protestant religion. Given that the queen had lent costumes to the City guilds for the pageants and that a full account of the procession was published in a propaganda pamphlet afterwards, there can be no doubt that the government had sponsored the event and influenced its content. Elizabeth's own actions during the procession also made this clear. Her quick-fire interjections, her general body language (smiles and nods), some of her more dramatic gestures, suggested that she knew what was coming and agreed with the message of the theatrical pieces. When, for example, she was presented with an English Bible, which had on it '*Verbum Veritatis*', the word of Truth, she ostentatiously kissed it, held it aloft, laid it

across her breast and thanked the City profusely. Elizabeth played her part well throughout the procession: not only did she know her script but she also showed herself to be confident on the public stage and relaxed in the company of her subjects.

The coronation service was less obviously Protestant than the eve of coronation procession. It could even be described as a liturgical hybrid. There were some Protestant elements: the all-night vigil on the eve of the coronation had been omitted; the Epistle and Gospel were said in English as well as Latin; and the consecrated elements were not elevated in the manner which implied their miraculous transform-ation into the body and blood of Christ. In consequence, the most senior of Mary's bishops refused to officiate, leaving the insignificant Bishop Oglethorpe of Carlisle to perform the coronation rites and the dean of the chapel royal to celebrate the mass. On the other hand, important Catholic features were retained, most notably the anointing of the monarch and the recitation of the traditional words of the mass. But Elizabeth could do no less: she was determined to work within the confines of the law and, until a new parliament sat and changed matters, Catholic worship was the only legal form in England.

Elizabeth's choice of councillors in the first months of her reign signalled that she was intending to make a clear break with the past. Twenty-nine of Mary's men lost their positions, including Lord Paget who was easily the most able, active and experienced. Of Mary's councillors who stayed in office, six were high status and powerful noblemen who could not be ignored, while the remaining four were useful second-ranking bureaucrats who had served under Edward VI as well as Mary. The nine new recruits were not political novices, despite their recent exclusion from power. With the exceptions of Sir Ambrose

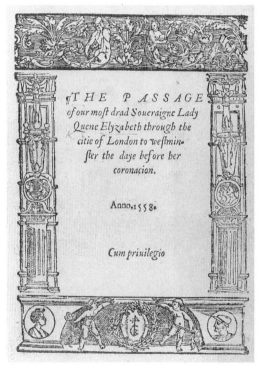

Cave and Thomas Parry, they had all worked as councillors or public servants under Edward VI, and only lost their positions when he died because of their Protestant beliefs. Two of them (the earl of Bedford and Sir Francis Knollys) had gone into exile to escape the Marian persecutions; the remainder were Nicodemites.

How did Elizabeth come to select these men? Since most of them were kinsmen, friends or associates of Cecil, it seems probable that she listened to and followed her secretary's advice at least in some cases. At the same time, though, a number of the new councillors had personal links with Elizabeth and we can see the queen's hand in their appointment. Richard Sackville was the first cousin of Anne Boleyn; Sir Francis Knollys's wife was Catherine Carey, Elizabeth's first cousin and long-time intimate; Parry was receiving his reward for long service (although he was only to enjoy it for a short while as he died in 1561). Sir Edward Rogers had been a member of her Hatfield household and imprisoned in the Tower because of his involvement in Wyatt's rebellion; no doubt his elevation to the post

William Cecil, Elizabeth's most trusted minister, whom she nicknamed her 'spirit'. This portrait was painted c. 1585, more than a decade after he had been elevated to the peerage as Baron Burghley. He then held the office of Lord Treasurer.
National Portrait Gallery

of vice-chamberlain in place of Sir Henry Bedingfield (Elizabeth's gaoler at Woodstock) appealed to the queen's sense of justice and humour. Overall, Elizabeth's council was much smaller than that of her predecessor, and it contained no clerics but was dominated by lay, well-educated and experienced public servants. She had chosen men whose loyalty she could trust and advice she would respect. She did not want 'yes' men; she might rail against a councillor's unwelcome advice but he would never be punished for it.

Elizabeth's most important minister until his death in 1598 was Sir William Cecil, elevated to become Baron Burghley in 1571. During the first thirteen years of the reign he acted both as her private secretary in charge of the stamp of her sign manual (to imprint her signature on letters and documents) and as secretary of state, organising and presiding over the meetings of the council whenever the queen was absent - which she usually was. He also gathered and evaluated information from spies, agents and ambassadors, drafted replies to letters and drew up policy options. Despite the frequent attacks of gout that laid him low, his capacity for work was immense, while his intelligence enabled him to carry out his multifarious tasks efficiently. Dedicated and effective public servant though he undoubtedly was, Cecil was as ambitious as any other politician and certainly not immune to corruption. Enormous sums of state revenue ended up in his private coffers. In character he was serious-minded, conventional, even a little pompous, rather like the figure of Polonius in Shakespeare's *Hamlet*. His relationship with Elizabeth was close and survived moments of intense conflict over policy. Thirteen years her senior, Cecil generally assumed an avuncular role, advising, cajoling but never bullying the queen into following his opinion. Traditionally, historians have viewed him as Elizabeth's natural partner, 'her spirit' (as she liked to call him), equally cautious, pragmatic and 'politique' as his mistress. Recently, however, historians have been seeing Cecil in a different light, more risk-taking, more radical in religion, and more ideological than his conservative monarch.

Two other men dominated political life in the 1560s but they were not brought into the council until October 1562. The first was Thomas Howard, fourth duke of Norfolk, who was the wealthiest and most powerful nobleman in the realm. As the premier peer, he was appointed earl marshal in 1558, a position which gave him responsibility for the ceremonial functions of monarchy. Not surprisingly he was highly conscious of his status and resented the 'new men' at court who possessed neither his lineage nor his family's record of service to the crown. His relations with Elizabeth were warm, though not intimate, but increasingly during the late 1560s she became suspicious of his intentions towards her rival, Mary Stewart.

The second dominating figure, by contrast, was Elizabeth's long-term favourite and the man she probably would have liked to marry: Robert Dudley. Dudley could easily have been dismissed by Norfolk as a 'a new man', for both his father (the duke of Northumberland) and grandfather (a minister of Henry VII) had been attainted for treason. Indeed Robert Dudley himself had been imprisoned for over a year in the Tower with his three surviving brothers as punishment for supporting Lady Jane Grey in July 1553. There is no hard evidence about the number or nature of his encounters with Elizabeth before her accession, although he later said that they had first met as children when she was eight years old. It is certainly likely that they met when he was a member of Prince Edward's household in the early 1540s. On her accession Elizabeth appointed Dudley as her master of the horse, a household office of distinction, which gave him responsibility for supervising the royal stables and opportunities to attend on the queen whenever she was out riding. In the early 1560s she showered titles, properties and money on him, elevating him in 1564 to the earldom of Leicester. Their relationship was sometimes stormy, but he remained at the centre of her emotional life until his death in September 1588. He was also a minister of substance, who helped shape her foreign policy and used his patronage in ways that influenced the nature of the Church, the universities and local government.

From the outset of her reign, the members of Elizabeth's household reflected her personal preferences, as she understandably wanted to have long-time friends, kinswomen, and the wives and daughters of her ministers and courtiers serving on her person. As a result, she cleared out Mary's household, leaving only about a dozen of Mary's fifty or so personal attendants to survive the purge; amongst them were Ladies Katherine and Mary Grey, Elizabeth's

cousins from the Suffolk line. Unsurprisingly, Kat Ashley was appointed chief
gentlewoman of the privy chamber, and her husband, John Ashley, was also
rewarded for his loyalty by his appointment as master of the jewel house and one
of the two gentlemen of the privy chamber. Blanche Parry, another old retainer,
became a gentlewoman of the bedchamber with close access to the queen as well
as keeper of the queen's jewels and books; after Kat's death in July 1565 she took
her place as chief gentlewoman. Castiglione, Elizabeth's Italian tutor who had
been arrested in 1556, was made a groom of the privy chamber, while William
St Loe, a servant arrested at the time of Wyatt's rebellion, was appointed captain
of the guard. In addition to trusted long-term servants Elizabeth also brought
her Howard and Boleyn kinswomen into the privy chamber, including Lady
Catherine Knollys, Katherine and Philadelphia Carey (the granddaughters of
Mary Boleyn), Mary Howard and Frances Radcliffe. Finally, the wives and
daughters of Elizabeth's new ministers and courtiers were not neglected: Mary
Lady Sidney (sister of Robert Dudley), Lady Howard of Effingham (the wife
of the lord chamberlain) and Lady Clinton (the wife of the lord admiral) were
amongst the elite women who staffed the privy chamber early in the reign.

Perhaps a dozen or so of the women who served Elizabeth had specific
tasks for which they received a salary but most of them were unsalaried, offering
their services to their monarch as an honour. Their role was to provide an
elegant backdrop to court life, to accompany the queen on ceremonial occasions,
and amuse her at other times with games and conversation. Elizabeth was
determined that they should remain outside politics, and those who disobeyed
this instruction were punished.

Elizabeth has acquired a reputation of being spiteful and cruel towards her
female servants, but this estimation is probably unfair. Certainly examples can be

found when she verbally abused or even physically assaulted them in an outburst of anger. But many of these incidents tended to be exaggerated in the telling by unreliable gossips, such as Bess of Hardwick or Sir John Harington. Most of the incidents also occurred later in the reign, when Elizabeth had become generally more irascible and intolerant. While there is no question that Elizabeth had a quick and fiery temper, her rages were almost always provoked by deceitful and disobedient behaviour. In the case of her ladies she became enraged when they married without permission or became pregnant by unsuitable men. There are many examples, however, of her helping her ladies secure a good marriage, enjoying their weddings, and allowing their return as married gentlewomen of the chamber. It should also not be forgotten how loyal and gracious she could be to her intimates and that the turnover of her household was very low. The majority of women served until death or severe illness intervened. When discharged because of ill-health, they received a good pension. Where possible they were usually succeeded by their daughters and granddaughters.

Shortly after her accession Elizabeth indicated that she planned to introduce religious change as soon as she possibly could. By Christmas 1558 she was listening to at least part of the services in the royal chapel in English, and on Christmas Day she ordered the officiating bishop not to elevate the host at high mass. He refused and Elizabeth theatrically 'rose and departed' at the end of the Gospel and thereafter would only attend mass when celebrated by her own chaplains without the elevation. A few days later, she issued a proclamation which permitted her subjects to hear the litany, Lord's Prayer and the Creed in English until parliament met and authorised other changes in the liturgy. At the opening of parliament on 30 January 1559, she also signalled that she would be introducing new statutes to reverse Mary's Catholic reformation. A Protestant married priest was chosen to preach at Westminster Abbey for the occasion, and his sermon, which would have been vetted by the government, attacked monasticism and idolatry. Elizabeth's own contempt for monasticism was publicly displayed when she brushed aside the monks leading the procession into the abbey with the words 'Away with these torches, for we see very well'.

The new Protestant settlement, however, was not secured without a struggle for there was stiff opposition in the House of Lords, particularly from the bishops who had been appointed under Mary. In the vain hope of conciliating them, Elizabeth agreed to abandon the title 'Supreme Head of the Church', which her father and brother had used, and to be called instead 'Supreme Governor'. The change of wording also appeased those Protestants who were deeply uncomfortable with the notion of a woman acting as the head of a Church in which only men were called to be apostles, evangelists and ministers. Elizabeth, however, justified the change on the grounds that 'this honour is due to Christ alone and cannot belong to any human being soever'. Despite relinquishing the title, she was determined to exercise the royal supremacy as forcefully as her father had done.

Elizabeth handed over the work of drawing up a new Protestant prayer book to a committee of divines who set to work on making minor revisions to the second prayer book that had been introduced in 1552 under Edward VI. The 1559 prayer book, which emerged from their discussions, nonetheless, reflected Elizabeth's own personal beliefs and ceremonial preferences. It was in English throughout, quoted extensively from scripture and incorporated Protestant doctrines on salvation and the sacraments. The communion service embodied Elizabeth's own understanding of the sacrament of the Lord's Supper. The officiating minister's words explicitly denied Catholic doctrines concerning the sacrificial nature of the sacrament and transubstantiation, but allowed for a belief in the physical presence of Christ in the bread and wine. The prayer book, moreover, retained ceremonials and practices liked by the queen but considered papist by many radical Protestants: communion was to be received kneeling; the minister was directed to make the sign of the cross over the baby in baptism; a ring would be exchanged during the marriage service; and most important of all, the priests had to wear a plain surplice at ordinary services and a cope at communion.

A few months later Elizabeth issued a set of royal injunctions setting out more detailed directives. Many of the articles protected the traditional features of the Church liked by the queen but targeted as 'popish' by more radical Protestants: elaborate church music, 'seemly habits' worn by priests, certain church furnishings, and ceremonies such as kneeling during the litany service and bowing at the name of Jesus. Additionally Elizabeth tried to enhance the mystery of the communion service by insisting that plain wafers should be offered by the minister in place of the ordinary bread specified in the prayer book. Although the Church in England was to be close to Calvinism in doctrine, its outward appearance was to retain Catholic features abhorred by Calvinists everywhere.

Over the next two years, Elizabeth again attempted to impose a restraining hand on the religious zeal of some of her subjects when she promulgated a number of proclamations which were designed to prevent their wilful destruction of funeral monuments, fonts and church bells. It should not be thought that her personal intervention was made just to conciliate Catholics at home and abroad. They would hardly have been conciliated by such cosmetic measures; besides, Elizabeth was obviously committed to the beauty of holiness for its own sake, believing traditional practices to be more appropriate for the mystery and majesty of divine worship and perfectly compatible with true religion as based on the scriptures.

Elizabeth's attempts to hold back the wholesale purification of the Church did not immediately alarm those Protestants who were hoping for the implementation of a programme of 'godly reform'. They surmised that Elizabeth would ignore diversity of practice when initiated by 'the godly' and come down hard on the disobedience of Catholics. They also assumed that she would introduce amendments to the prayer book and further reform as soon as the international situation was less threatening. They were wrong. In the mid-1560s, Elizabeth insisted on conformity to the prayer book and injunctions, and exhorted her first archbishop of Canterbury, Matthew Parker, to correct and punish all ministers who refused to follow its directives. Although many ministers reluc-

tantly conformed, a number of them became embittered by the campaign to enforce obedience, and began to question or challenge the right of the bishops to govern the Church. On the other hand, it seems likely that the vast majority

MARIE
REINE
D'ESCOS-
SE

of the populace were relieved that the queen and bishops were protecting many
of their familiar rituals and traditional religious practices from the attacks of
Protestant zealots. As it was, many parishioners were dismayed at the disappearance
of the mass and removal of images from their churches. Undoubtedly some of
them hoped that Elizabeth would take a Catholic husband and return to Rome
or that she might shortly die to be succeeded by a Catholic heir.

As well as imposing a new religious settlement on England, Elizabeth
had to deal with a difficult international situation. At the time of her accession
diplomats were already in the process of negotiating a peace treaty with France,
but Elizabeth was very reluctant to start the reign with the formal surrender of
Calais, which the French were determined to keep. But with no resources to
fight for its re-conquest, Elizabeth could only haggle for face-saving terms. At last
in April 1559 she accepted the best on offer: England would not cede sovereignty
of Calais but would allow the French to occupy it for eight years and then they
would either return the territory or pay an indemnity.

Despite this agreement, a permanent peace with France looked unlikely in
1559. New tensions over dynasty and religion were operating to keep alive the
traditional hostility between England and her long-standing enemy. In the first
place the young French dauphin, who became King Francis II of France in July
1559, was the husband of Mary Stewart, the titular queen of Scotland and the
Catholic claimant to the English throne. Consequently, many English politicians
feared, with some justification, that the French would invade England through
Scotland in order to place Mary on Elizabeth's throne. In the second place,
Calvinism was spreading into both France and Scotland, and making converts
amongst powerful noblemen who looked to Elizabeth as their protector against
the French authorities threatening to destroy them.

The first crisis came in late 1559 when the Scottish Calvinist nobles appealed to Elizabeth for help against their regent, Mary of Guise, the French-born mother of Mary Stewart who was ruling Scotland during her daughter's absence in France. Instinctively, Elizabeth had no wish to intervene. She was unwilling to be publicly associated with rebels and, besides, she hated John Knox, the spiritual leader of the Scottish Calvinists, because of his recently published pamphlet denouncing female rule. Yet, she could not ignore the danger to her crown. If French expeditionary forces arrived in Scotland to suppress heresy, the army could turn against England once it had completed its work against the Scottish nobles. As a result Elizabeth agreed to send ships to blockade the Firth of Forth where the French army was expected to land. Initially, however, she refused to send an English army into Scotland to pre-empt a French attack. It was only when Cecil threatened to resign from all responsibility for Scottish affairs if she did not intervene there that she reluctantly ordered the duke of Norfolk northwards to head an army for use in Scotland.

Over the next five months, Elizabeth found herself nudged into making ever more military commitments to her Scottish allies, until in May 1560 her troops made an assault on Leith, the port just outside Edinburgh then held by a French garrison. When the attempt failed with the estimated loss of a thousand men, Elizabeth was furious: 'I have had such a torment herein with the Queen's Majesty as an ague hath not in five fits so much abated', complained Cecil. Luckily the French wanted peace because of difficulties they were facing at home from their own Calvinist subjects, and Elizabeth was soon able to disentangle herself from the war with her honour intact and original objectives achieved. By the terms of the Treaty of Edinburgh (July 1560) it was agreed that the French would evacuate all their troops from Scotland and that Mary Stewart would

In July 1563 the remnants of the
English army surrendered and returned
home, bringing the plague with them.
Calais was irretrievably lost...

neither bear the title nor quarter the arms of England, as she had until then been doing in France. In many ways this success was the work of Cecil rather than Elizabeth. It was he who had persuaded her to act, restrained her from pulling out when the going got hard, and successfully negotiated the final treaty.

In October 1562 Elizabeth embarked on a second campaign abroad. It was to be the only occasion during her whole reign when she felt any enthusiasm for military adventure, but the project was ill-conceived, and the outcome a military and political fiasco. In France, the Huguenots (the name given to French Calvinists) were on the defensive against the militant Catholics and sought the aid of fellow Protestants abroad including Elizabeth. She was tempted to provide military help after they had offered her the port of Le Havre in Normandy to be exchanged for Calais at the end of a victorious campaign. No doubt, Elizabeth was encouraged to be adventurous by the success of the earlier Scottish war. The most outspoken of her councillors, moreover, were behind a policy of military intervention, favouring it for religious or strategic reasons, while from outside the council Robert Dudley promoted the Huguenot cause with vigour because he wanted to make his mark as a military man. The venture was a terrible mistake. The Huguenots soon abandoned their English allies and joined with the French royal army to move against Le Havre where an English garrison was holed up and soon dying from the plague. In July 1563 the remnants of the English army surrendered and returned home, bringing the plague with them. Calais was irretrievably lost as the French now refused to pay the compensation they had promised in the 1559 treaty, and Elizabeth learned her lesson from this debacle. During the 1570s she resisted the advice of councillors that she send military assistance to Protestants abroad who were in rebellion against their rulers. It was not until 1585 that she ordered another English army to fight in Europe.

4

'And in the end this shall be for me
sufficient, that a marble stone shall
declare that a Queen, having reigned
such a time, lived and died a virgin'.

Marriage and succession 1558–68

For Elizabeth's subjects there were good reasons to want their queen to marry.
Protestants obviously hoped that a married queen would give birth to a
Protestant heir who would continue to uphold the new religious settlement, and
they feared that, if she remained single and barren, Catholic contenders would
jockey for power during her lifetime and fight for the throne on her death.
English Catholics, too, preferred Elizabeth to marry for they were equally fearful
that a war of succession would follow the death of a childless Elizabeth.
Furthermore they anticipated that Elizabeth would marry a Catholic prince and
that he would influence her to grant religious toleration at home or better still
to return the country to Rome.

There was no shortage of candidates for Elizabeth's hand at the beginning
of the reign: some were English (such as the earl of Arundel and Robert Dudley)
but most of them were foreign (including Philip II of Spain, Eric XIV of Sweden
and Archduke Charles of Austria). A few pursued their suits with vigour,
others without evident enthusiasm. Amongst the latter was Philip II who only
grudgingly offered his hand for the sake of true religion and was clearly relieved
when Elizabeth refused him for pretty much the same reason. On the other
hand, Eric was a most persistent suitor. In the summer of 1559 his father, King
Gustavus, sent an embassy to England with a matrimonial proposal for Elizabeth.
While the leading envoys stressed the political advantages of the match, the
Swedes in their retinue wore livery 'displaying some hearts pierced by a javelin
on the lapels of their red velvet coats symbolising the passion of their sovereign'.
A few months later, Gustavus dispatched his younger son Duke John of Finland
to the English court to make a good impression on the queen and plead his
brother's suit. John carried out his assignment admirably: during his seven-month
stay in London, he impressed the court with his 'very civil and modest behaviour'

...to determyne... tyme... wherwth the Realme may or shall haue
iuste cause to be discontented And therfore put that [therout?] out of
your hedes. ffor I assure yo[u] what credditt my assuraunce may haue
wth yo[u] I do not well tell but what creditt it shall deserue to haue
the sequel shall declare. I will never in that matter conclude any
thinge that shalbe preiudiciall to the realme. ffor the [wele?] good
& saftie wherof I will never shame to spend my life And whensomever
my chaunce shalbe to light apon [it?] trust ye shalbe as carefull for
the realme and yo[u] I will not saie as my self because I do not
so [arrontlie?] determyne of any other but at the least wayes, by my
good will and desire, he shalbe suche as shalbe as carefull for
the preseruacion of the realme and yo[u] as my self. And albeit it
might please almightie god to contynew me still in this mynde, to
lyue out of the state of mariage, yet it is not to be feared, but he
will so [worke?] in my harte, and in yo[u] wisdomes as good prouision
by his helpe may be made in convenient tyme wherby the realme
shall not remayne destitute of an heire [that] may be a fitt gouernor
and parabenture more beneficiall to the realme then suche offspring
as may come of me. ffor although I be never so carefull of yo[ur]
wele doinge and mynd ever so to be, yit it may me issue [I?] [haue?]
out of kynde, and become parhappe vngracious. And in the
ende this shalbe for me sufficient that a marble stone shall declare... [at my death?]... a [Queen?]... [virgin?]
...beseginn... doe here I end & take yo[ur] doinge [vnto?]... good
[parte?], and giue [vnto?] yo[u] all [efftones?] my hartie thankes, more yit
for yo[ur] zeale & good meaning then for yo[ur] [petition?]

and lavish spending on hospitality, gifts, even doles to the poor. By the time he eventually left England he had won many friends but not Elizabeth's acceptance of his brother's proposal. Nonetheless Eric was not daunted. After sending his chancellor to the English court in early 1561 with another marriage proposal, he made plans to come in person to meet the queen. The weather however defeated him. Setting out from Sweden with thirty or so ships, he was twice beaten back by strong storms and only three ships reached England, one of them containing twenty-four horses six of which had died on board for want of drinking water. The surviving horses were stabled in London for public display while the bullion on the ships was unloaded at the Tower. Even after this misfortune, Eric continued to pester the queen but, in reality, the life had gone from his courtship and the following year he was looking elsewhere for a royal bride.

Elizabeth did not string along her suitors as part of a diplomatic game. She told all the foreign princes who asked for her hand in 1559 and 1560 that she had chosen, for the time being, to remain single, although she had not closed her mind to marriage entirely. As she explained in February 1559 to the members of her parliament who petitioned her to marry, she had until that time been content to lead a single life though God might in future 'incline my heart to another kind of life'. If he did, she continued, 'you may well assure yourselves my meaning is not to do or determine anything wherewith the realm may or shall have just cause to be discontented'. Her choice of husband, she promised, would be 'for the weal, good and safety' of the realm. She concluded with her most memorable words: 'And in the end this shall be for me sufficient, that a marble stone shall declare that a Queen, having reigned such a time, lived and died a virgin'.

Neither Philip nor Eric nor numerous other suitors inclined Elizabeth's heart to marry in 1559 or early 1560, but at times over the next few years she did

When I was fayre & yoge then favour graced me
Of many was I sought their mystres for to be
But I did scorne them all & answerds them therfore
Go go go seeke some other where importune me no more
How many wepinge eyes I made to pine in woe
How many sytchyng hartes I have not skyll to shoe
But I the prowder grew and still thys spake therfore
Go go go seeke some other where importune me no more
Then spake fayre venus sonne ý brave victorioal Boy
Saying yow daynty dame for ý yow be so coy
I wll so pull yowr plumes as yow shall say no more
Go go go eke some other where importune me no more
As he had sayd such chayge grew in my brest
That neyther moht nor lay I could take any rest
Wherfore I did repent ý I had sayd befor
Go go go seke som other where importune me no more

FINIS . ELy .

consider entering 'another kind of life'. She came to prefer the prospect of marriage to the more dangerous device of naming an heir to settle the succession. Duty moreover began to mingle with desire when her virile master of the horse, Robert Dudley, became free to marry after his wife's mysterious death in September 1560.

Elizabeth's attraction to Dudley started to be noticed as early as April 1559. Soon afterwards comments about their relationship began to become defamatory. Since Lady Amy Dudley did not live at court, it was reported that Elizabeth visited her husband in his chamber at all hours, that they were lovers, and that they would marry once Amy died. Kat Ashley was so distressed by the damage incurred to Elizabeth's reputation – not for the first time – that 'she implored her in God's name to marry [someone else] and put an end to all these disreputable rumours'. Elizabeth self-righteously tried to dismiss her servant's concerns; the constant presence of her ladies, she said, gave a lie to the gossip and it was unfair that she should be so calumnied, lamenting that 'in this world she had so much sorrow and tribulation and so little joy'. Elizabeth's response was understandable but naïve: as a woman, her honour depended on sexual purity; as the daughter of Anne Boleyn, her reputation was fragile; and with a history of sexual slander

Opposite: Robert Dudley, earl of
Leicester, Elizabeth's favourite and
suitor for her hand. He entered her
council in 1563 and she nicknamed
him her 'eyes'.
National Portrait Gallery

already behind her she could not afford to provoke further accusations of
wantonness.

On 8 September 1560, Amy Dudley was found with her neck broken at
the bottom of a short flight of eight stairs in the house where she was staying
at Cumnor near Oxford. She was alone at the time, and the most reasonable
explanation for the fall is that she committed suicide. As soon as she heard the
news, Elizabeth realised that Dudley would come under suspicion of murder and
she immediately sent him away from court to his house in Kew until an inquest
had been held to clear his name. Her action, however, did not stem the flow of
rumours that poured forth over the next few months. In England and abroad
people from all social groups were saying that Dudley had murdered his wife to
marry the queen, and some were also suggesting that Elizabeth was an accessory
to the fact. Dudley's attempt to play the role of the grieving widower – the grand
funeral he supplied for his wife and his donning of mourning clothes for six
months – were condemned as hypocrisy, and few believed the verdict of the
coroner's court that Amy had died accidentally. In these circumstances it was
impossible for Elizabeth to marry her favourite and retain her honour, or even
possibly her throne.

No letters or records exist to tell us how Elizabeth was feeling in the
months after Amy's death. She certainly showed signs of emotional strain, and
a messenger who travelled to and from the court reported in late November
1560 that she looked 'not so hearty and well as she did by a great deal'. For a
time she seemed undecided about the outlook for her relationship with Dudley.
At one point she drew up a patent for ennobling him, a promotion that was a
prerequisite for any marriage, but when it was ready for her signature she slashed
the document with a knife in some distress. At no time, though, did she waver in

her support for her favourite, and anyone who openly disparaged him was in danger of disgrace or detention. In all probability she wanted to marry him but was grappling with the recognition that the serious slur on his name made the union impossible, especially as most of her nobility and councillors were opposed to the match.

In January 1561 Dudley decided on a bold move to improve his fortunes. Through an intermediary he approached the Spanish ambassador to ask if Philip would back his marriage to the queen. His messenger intimated that in return he would arrange for English representatives to attend the general council of the Church summoned by the pope to meet at Trent in Italy. The Spanish ambassador was flabbergasted, but prepared to listen, and over the next few months tried to use Dudley to influence the queen in the Catholic interest. Elizabeth knew of these negotiations but it is difficult to know what she made of them. In any event Cecil sabotaged them. By inciting an anti-Catholic scare he closed the door to the queen agreeing to any action that might persuade Philip to promote the match with Dudley. By the summer of 1561 Elizabeth's emotional crisis was evidently over. Her mood lightened, and she could even afford to jest with the Spanish ambassador that he could act as a minister at her wedding to her favourite if only he could speak English. Dudley did not entirely abandon his hopes, but the tide had turned against his ever becoming the queen's consort. Whether or not he was ever the queen's lover is unknown, but seems unlikely, not least because Elizabeth appears far too cautious a character to risk exposure through a pregnancy.

In October 1562 Elizabeth suddenly fell dangerously ill with smallpox. During the emergency, the court and council were in total disarray about the succession. According to the Spanish ambassador, they split three ways: some supported Lady Katherine Grey, others the earl of Huntingdon (from the Yorkist line) and a third group wanted to consult the opinion of lawyers who were believed to favour the claim of Mary Stewart. Thinking she was on her deathbed Elizabeth came up with the unrealistic – indeed bizarre – solution that Dudley should be made Protector of England, whatever that meant! Incidentally, she also declared that although she loved Dudley dearly, as God was her witness nothing improper had ever taken place between them. Luckily Elizabeth recovered, but those active in the political life of the nation were badly shaken. Consequently, during the parliamentary session of 1563, members of parliament petitioned the queen to marry or, if not, to follow the precedent of her father and lay down the succession in a parliamentary statute. Cecil had a more radical solution to the problem. In an abortive bill, he proposed that on the queen's death sovereignty would be temporarily invested in the council so that it could deal with all matters of state until a new parliament chose a new monarch. Elizabeth, however, swept aside any such proposals. She forbade parliament to discuss the succession but assured it that she would look for a husband: despite her preference as a private woman for a life of celibacy, she declared, 'I strive with myself to think it not meet for a prince. And if I can bend my liking to your need I will not resist such a mind'.

As Elizabeth was thinking to marry 'as a prince' and not for private pleasure, she decided to choose a man of royal blood from abroad as her consort. By this time, however, all her previous foreign suitors had melted away and it was left to Cecil and his agents to seek out a suitable candidate. Cecil's eye fell on Archduke Charles of Austria, the son of the Holy Roman Emperor and first cousin to Philip II. Charles was thought a good match in terms of age, royal lineage and the alliance he would bring with the whole Habsburg clan in

Europe, an alliance which would enhance England's commercial interests and act as a protective mantle against France and Scotland. His main disadvantage – his Catholic religion – was not thought to be an insuperable barrier; Cecil argued that there would be no danger to English Protestantism as long as the archduke and his retainers did not practise their religion openly in England. Elizabeth, too, could see the advantages of marrying a Habsburg prince but she had little enthusiasm for the project. Apart from other considerations, she had heard that Charles was deformed and ugly. Perhaps with the memory of her father's disastrous marriage to the unattractive Anne of Cleves in mind, she insisted that he visit her in England before a marriage was agreed. Yet despite her reservations, Elizabeth announced – indeed for the first time in her life – that 'she was now resolved to marry' and gave as her reason 'the insistent pressure that was brought to bear on her by the Estates of her realm'.

It took until 1565 for the Austrians to respond positively to Cecil's proposal and send a diplomat to England to negotiate the match. In 1559 they had wasted time in promoting a match between Elizabeth and Charles, and they now needed to be convinced of the queen's sincerity. When an Austrian envoy eventually arrived at court, Elizabeth showed that she was serious about marriage by delegating responsibility for negotiating a matrimonial treaty to her inner council, comprising Cecil, Norfolk and Dudley (who was now the earl of Leicester). They could not, however, reach an agreement on several central issues, the most important of which concerned religion. The Austrians insisted that the archduke should be excused from English church services and permitted to attend a public mass, but Elizabeth found this demand unacceptable. She explained that a concession of this kind would encourage English Catholics to disobey the law and would destabilise the realm by encouraging her subjects

'I have always abhorred to draw in question the title of the crown,' she explained, 'so many disputes have been already touching it in the mouths of men'.

to expect a change in religion. Not surprisingly therefore, the negotiations faltered and the Austrian envoy went home disappointed.

A year later the thirty-three-year-old Elizabeth re-opened the negotiations. Her parliament of 1566 had proved difficult to manage because of its efforts to force her to marry or name a successor, and she felt compelled to act on the marriage front to silence the criticisms of MPs. Although she probably had little expectation that the Austrians would change their position on religion, she dispatched a leading supporter of the match, the earl of Sussex, to Vienna in June 1567 to discuss terms directly with the emperor. Sussex proved an able negotiator and the Austrians made two important concessions: the archduke would accompany the queen to English church services, and no longer demand a public mass provided that he could hear mass privately in his own room. When Elizabeth brought this demand to her councillors, they divided on the issue: Cecil and Norfolk were amongst those who supported the match on these terms but Leicester and Sir Francis Knollys led the opposition to it. Meanwhile, outside the council other voices spoke out against a Catholic mass being celebrated again in England. Elizabeth was therefore left in no doubt that marriage to the archduke on the terms he required would be extremely unpopular with her most zealously Protestant subjects. Furthermore, she was only too aware in 1567 that an unpopular marriage could seriously damage her political power, for she had before her the example of Mary Stewart. Only six months earlier the Scottish queen had faced an armed rebellion and been forced to abdicate as a direct result of her controversial marriage to the earl of Bothwell. In these circumstances Elizabeth decided to play it safe, probably with a huge sigh of relief!

With Elizabeth now unlikely to marry and bear a child, who would be her successor? In the mid-1560s there were at least eight possible candidates, with two clear favourites: Mary Stewart, Queen of Scotland, and Katherine Grey. Mary Stewart possessed the best hereditary claim as she was the granddaughter of Henry VIII's older sister, Margaret, by her first marriage to James V of Scotland. Her title, however, had been weakened by Henry's decision to leave out any mention of the Scottish line in his will, and her detractors also argued that she could not inherit English lands and titles since she was born an alien. It was, however, her religion, not her nationality, that made Mary an unacceptable queen to many Protestants, including Cecil, who feared she would re-introduce Catholic worship into England. She was also strongly distrusted because of her family links with the leading Catholic faction in France and her unwillingness to renounce her claim to the English throne while Elizabeth was living.

Katherine Grey was the choice of most Protestants. She was the granddaughter of Henry VIII's younger sister, Mary, which meant that her title by blood was weaker than that of her cousin Mary Stewart. But, Katherine's supporters could claim that she had a stronger legal right to the throne, because first Henry had privileged her family line in his will and second she had been born in England. Katherine, however, ruined her political prospects by entering into a clandestine marriage with Edward Seymour, earl of Hertford, son of the late Lord Protector Somerset. Both as a lady of the privy chamber and a royal heiress, Katherine required the queen's permission to wed and indeed risked an accusation of treason in marrying without it. Nonetheless the couple went ahead without the queen's consent since they believed, not unreasonably, that it would not be forthcoming. Their secret marriage took place in late 1560 but could not remain concealed for long. Katherine conceived quickly and had to confess her condition the following August when she was eight months pregnant.

Elizabeth's reaction to the news was predictable. She was 'much offended' at the deceit, and ordered the lovers to be sent to the Tower. There in September 1561 Katherine gave birth to a son, which caused Elizabeth still more anguish, for the sex of the child strengthened his mother's claim to be Elizabeth's heir and might also encourage revolts in his name by disaffected subjects. To protect herself from these dangers, Elizabeth was determined to have the baby pronounced a bastard and with this end in view she appointed an ecclesiastical commission to investigate the validity of his parents' marriage. Katherine made it easy for Elizabeth. Displaying staggering ineptitude, she had lost the documentation that would prove her marriage valid and had even failed to learn the name of the officiating priest. In a stroke of bad luck, moreover, the one other witness to the ceremony had died. An ecclesiastical commission, therefore, was able to declare that no marriage had taken place and that Katherine's son was consequently illegitimate. But Elizabeth's troubles were not over. Thanks to the leniency of the lieutenant of the Tower, who allowed Hertford to make secret conjugal visits to his wife, a second son was born to the couple in February 1563. A strong case could be made that this child was legitimate given that his parents had publicly exchanged vows before the ecclesiastical commission. Elizabeth, however, would have none of it. She imposed a further fine on Hertford for his 'illicit and illegitimate carnal copulation', and ensured that the lovers never saw each other again. Though removed from the Tower, Katherine was kept under house arrest until her death in January 1568.

Some of Elizabeth's biographers believed her treatment of the Seymour family was unnecessarily harsh and vindictive, and suggested that it was motivated both by her personal dislike of the whole Grey family and emotional distress at having had to relinquish her own desire to marry Dudley. Katherine's sheer incompetence demonstrated that her motivation was romantic love not political ambition, while her well-reported distress at her separation from her husband moved many others to pity. But Katherine's personal happiness was far less important to Elizabeth than her own political safety and the succession was a highly sensitive issue. Hertford's uncle, Lord Thomas Seymour, had sought to marry a royal heiress to enhance his power and status, and it was reasonable to suppose that his nephew was acting out of the same motive. Furthermore, the lovers had shown themselves to be disobedient to their sovereign and unworthy of her trust. It is possible that Elizabeth might in time have forgiven Katherine and set her at liberty, but Hertford kept trying to prove his marriage legal while his supporters wrote pamphlets defending the right of his sons to inherit the throne.

Elizabeth showed a little more compassion to Katherine's younger sister Lady Mary Grey, who in 1565 married also without royal permission. Although her husband, Thomas Keyes, was imprisoned in London's Fleet Prison for a few years, Mary was merely ordered to live under supervision in certain country houses. After his death in 1572, moreover, she had complete freedom of movement and set up her own house in London, even attending court occasionally in 1578, the year of her death. Elizabeth could afford to be more charitable in this case, however, since Mary Grey had never been a political threat. As a dwarf who was 'crookbacked and very ugly', she was hardly a serious contender to be queen while her marriage to a man six foot eight inches tall, and her social inferior to boot, entirely ruled her out of the succession.

Of the many claimants to the succession, Elizabeth herself favoured Mary Stewart. Not surprisingly Elizabeth felt a strong sense of rivalry with her royal cousin and feared her pretensions to the English throne, but she still believed that Mary had the best right by blood to rule after her. Nonetheless, she would not designate Mary (nor later her son James born in 1566) as her heir for a number of sound reasons. In the first place she knew her subjects were divided over the succession: 'I have always abhorred to draw in question the title of the crown,' she explained, 'so many disputes have been already touching it in the mouths of men'. Naming Mary therefore would not settle the issue but open it up. It would, moreover, be unpopular with many Protestants and alienate Elizabeth from Cecil and other councillors she valued, who were implacably opposed to Mary's succession. Besides, it was doubtful whether a bill that put Mary next in line for the throne could ever pass through a Protestant House of Commons. Even without these practical considerations Elizabeth was opposed to naming a successor for fear that it would undermine her own power. As she explained to a Scottish ambassador in 1561: 'it is to be feared that if they [my subjects] knew a certain successor of our crown they would have recourse thither'. Drawing on her own experience during the previous reign, she believed that an heir presumptive might become the focus of plots or the centre of an alternative court while she was still alive.

5

... those unhappy with the religious
changes kept their heads down and
waited for better times.

Plots, peace and Protestants 1568–88

During the 1560s, Elizabeth's Catholic subjects were generally quiescent. The bishops who refused to take the oath of supremacy, which recognised the queen as Supreme Governor of the Church, left their posts quietly and did not lead Catholic resistance to the new Protestant settlement. The vast majority of the parish clergy who had implemented the Catholic measures of Mary I continued in their posts under her sister, while conservative lay people went to church on Sundays in accordance with the Act of Uniformity introduced in 1559. English Catholics were under no great pressure to withdraw their obedience from the queen because the pope neither issued a bull of excommunication nor called for a crusade against Elizabeth. Consequently those unhappy with the religious changes kept their heads down and waited for better times.

Elizabeth had no wish to persecute those of her Catholic subjects who obeyed the law. Provided that they attended Protestant services and went without the mass, she had no interest in setting up inquisitions to determine whether or not they believed correct doctrine. She was confident that, over time, exposure to Protestant worship, homilies and catechisms would lead them to 'true religion' without any need for coercion or an extensive missionary effort. In this approach she differed from most of her senior clergy and many of her councillors. On occasion, therefore, she had to intervene to protect her Catholic subjects from repressive legislation. After her 1563 Parliament legislated that the death penalty should be imposed on anyone who twice refused to take the oath of supremacy, she directed her bishops to offer it only once with the result that no-one was executed. In 1571, moreover, she used her royal veto to prevent a parliamentary bill which would have made participation in communion compulsory.

Nonetheless, Catholics were gradually frozen out of political life. The 1563 Treason Act required all members of the House of Commons to swear the oath

Elizabeth Regina.

2. PARALIPOM. 6.
¶ *Domine Deus Israel, non est similis tui Deus in cælo & in
terra, qui pacta custodis & misericordiam cum [servis] tuis,
qui ambulant coram te in toto corde suo.*

Previous page: Elizabeth preferred prayer to sermons as an expression of piety. On this frontispiece to Richard Day's *Christian Prayers and Meditations* in English, French, Italian, Spanish, Greek, and Latin, she is shown in prayer with her crown, sword of state and sceptre within close reach.
The British Library, C 24 a10

Opposite: In this proclamation of 1569, the earls of Northumberland and Westmorland called upon the men of the north 'to resort' to them with arms. Although they presented themselves as 'the Queen's most true and lawful subjects', their aim was probably to put Mary Queen of Scots on the throne.
The British Library, Harley MS 6990, f.90

of supremacy and thereafter it became increasingly Protestant in complexion. In a few shires, Catholic justices of the peace were no longer called to the bench, while in the north Protestants generally took up the positions of power and prominence that had been previously held by Catholic gentry or nobility. The earl of Northumberland, for example, lost his important military position as warden of the east and middle march on the borders with Scotland, while the Dacres family lost control of the west march in 1563. Consequently, the Catholic nobility in the north of England felt aggrieved that they, 'the ancient nobility', were losing influence to 'diverse new set up nobles' about the queen, and they pinned their hopes on a future regime led by Mary Stewart.

Mary Stewart, though, had her own problems. In 1567 her second husband, Henry Darnley, was murdered and shortly afterwards she married James Hepburn, the fourth earl of Bothwell, one of the men believed to be responsible for the deed. As a result, many in Scotland became convinced that Mary had been part of the plot to kill Darnley, and the Scottish Protestant lords raised an army against her. After defeat at the battle of Carberry Hill, Mary was forced to abdicate in favour of her thirteen-month-old son, James, and she was incarcerated in the island castle of Lochleven. The following May, she escaped but, after her supporters were defeated in battle, she fled in panic across the Solway Firth to England in the hope that she would receive sympathy and support from her cousin. To her genuine surprise none was forthcoming.

Elizabeth did not, however, revel in the difficulties of her rival. On the contrary, she had been so outraged at Mary's imprisonment the previous year that she had threatened armed intervention and refused to recognise either James VI as king of Scotland or the authority of his regent. With this new crisis Elizabeth again felt that Mary, as a kinswoman and fellow monarch, deserved her support, even though she was perturbed at her cousin's possible involvement in the death of Darnley and deplored her scandalous marriage to Bothwell. At the same time, however, Elizabeth appreciated that inviting the royal refugee to her court would imperil her own position. Furthermore she had no wish to alienate the new Scottish government, which was largely composed of Protestants, by favouring their deposed queen. Elizabeth consequently suppressed her first instinct to be generous to her cousin. Following the advice of Cecil, she refused to meet her and decided instead to hold her in a northern stronghold while she considered her future.

Elizabeth's preferred solution to the problem of Mary was her restoration to the Scottish throne on terms that would safeguard English interests. What Elizabeth wanted was a settlement whereby Mary would retain her sovereignty but an anglophile Scottish council would effectively rule her realm. As a first step to this end, Elizabeth offered to mediate between the Scottish queen and her rebellious subjects by holding a conference which would establish whether or not Mary had been an accessory to Darnley's murder, as the Scots claimed. If Mary were acquitted of the charge, she could be restored to her throne on Elizabeth's terms; if found guilty, Elizabeth would be justified in holding her under restraint in England. Cecil agreed with this process but, whereas Elizabeth apparently wanted an acquittal, Cecil preferred to see a verdict of guilty that would be followed by Mary's perpetual imprisonment in England.

In the event there was no final verdict. As Mary was denied permission to attend the judicial proceedings that opened in September 1568, her team refused to present any defence and effectively withdrew from the trial. Without hearing Mary's side of the argument Elizabeth felt unable to deliver a judgement. Nonetheless the evidence against Mary presented at the conference (the notorious 'Casket letters') was so compelling that it badly damaged her reputation in England, particularly amongst the councillors and noblemen who had been summoned to hear the case. Elizabeth now had good grounds for refusing to meet Mary, a woman who had failed to clear her name and therefore remained accused of a heinous crime. Elizabeth also felt it safe to let her disgraced cousin languish in detention at least for the time being.

In reality Mary's presence in England unsettled the political stability of the realm. With the death of Katherine Grey and the bastardisation of the Seymour boys, Mary had emerged as the strongest contender for the succession. After the breakdown of the Archduke Charles's matrimonial negotiations, moreover, it looked unlikely that Elizabeth would ever marry. In these circumstances, Catholics began to view Mary as their prospective saviour, while some Protestants thought they needed to open contact with her and prepare for the day when she might be queen of England. Amongst the latter was the duke of Norfolk who became embroiled in a scheme to marry Mary, a project supported by a wide assortment of courtiers and councillors including Leicester. Norfolk and his adherents were not envisaging treason but thought of the marriage as a means to convert Mary to Protestantism and resolve the succession question, but their secret negotiations were a breach of trust and source of danger to Elizabeth. Consequently when Leicester eventually confessed the intrigues to Elizabeth in September 1569, she was very angry indeed and forbade Norfolk to meddle in any scheme to marry Mary. Had Norfolk not then departed without leave for his house in Kenninghall, the seat of his power in East Anglia, this particular crisis would probably have fizzled out. But his flight sparked off the only major rebellion of Elizabeth's reign, the 'Northern Rebellion' led by the earls of Northumberland and Westmorland. Both earls had been privy to Norfolk's matrimonial plan, and mistakenly assumed that his flight to Norfolk was the signal for a general rising on behalf of Mary.

The Northern Rebellion which began in November 1569 was quickly suppressed. Warned that she could not trust the loyalty of the gentlemen living in the north of England, Elizabeth acted decisively and ordered northwards a southern army of some 10,000 men. By the time it arrived, however, the main rebellion had already collapsed. When a secondary rising under Lord Dacres erupted in January 1570, the rebel army was decimated by a far smaller force raised by Lord Hunsdon, the governor of Berwick. The rebel leaders fled to Scotland, but Northumberland was handed back and executed in 1572 while Westmorland and Dacres escaped to the Spanish Netherlands. The lesser participants had no such escape. Elizabeth had decided upon harsh reprisals and demanded that none of 'the meaner sort of rebels' should be spared. As a result some 500 of the 6,000 or so insurgents were hanged under martial law, and another 200 were condemned, only escaping the death penalty through the compassion of the men on the spot. Had Elizabeth had her way, everyone whose

Thomas Howard, the fourth duke of Norfolk, the premier peer of the realm, who was executed for treason in June 1572 after his involvement in a plot to depose Elizabeth.
Bridgeman Art Library

loyalty had been suspect would have been severely punished.

Elizabeth was unquestionably badly shaken by the Northern Rebellion, hence her merciless reaction. A papal bull of excommunication, which followed hard on its heels in February 1570 and was timed to coincide with it, did nothing to put her mind at rest, as the bull absolved English Catholics from their duty of allegiance to her. The uncovering of another plot in 1571 further demonstrated the vulnerability of her position. This latter conspiracy involved English noblemen, including Norfolk, who had been recently released from the Tower, Mary Stewart, Philip II, and a papal agent Roberto Ridolfi. The plan was for Elizabeth to be assassinated, for Norfolk and his friends to kindle a Catholic revolt, and for a small Spanish army to invade England from the Netherlands and to march on London. Luckily for Elizabeth, Ridolfi was such an inept conspirator that at least one historian has suspected him of being a double agent. During interrogations, Mary admitted giving Ridolfi a financial commission but strongly denied any other part in the scheme.

These Catholic activities against Elizabeth during the crisis of 1569 to 1571 had important repercussions. First they resulted in the removal of Norfolk, the premier English peer, from the political scene. He was convicted of treason in January 1572 but, in marked contrast to her eagerness to have the 'meaner sort of rebels' executed after the Northern Rebellion, Elizabeth hesitated several times before finally agreeing to Norfolk's death the following June. Second, the Ridolfi

Plot condemned the twenty-nine-year-old Mary to a life of exile and captivity. Although Elizabeth would not succumb to the pressure from members of her parliament who were baying for Mary's blood, she immediately ceased to work for the Scottish queen's restoration and permitted the publication of the evidence implicating her in Darnley's murder. Third, a crackdown on Catholics was initiated and justified on the grounds that they could no longer be trusted. The 1571 Parliament passed bills that made it treason for anyone to hold papal documents or to 'imagine' or intend the death or deposition of the queen, and over the next two decades increasingly draconian measures ensued. Furthermore, prominent Catholics were removed from the bench of magistrates and other local positions. Finally, because of Philip II's readiness to assist the northern earls and initiate plots with disaffected English Catholics, England's relations with Spain deteriorated further. The exposure of the Ridolfi Plot was soon followed by a defensive alliance with France against Spain.

Over the next ten years no significant plots were hatched within England which involved Mary Stewart directly. Aware that she was under close supervision and her correspondence was being monitored, she avoided intrigues with English or foreign Catholics against Elizabeth. Instead she concentrated on embroidery and letter writing; this latter activity for the purpose of securing her liberty and obtaining property she claimed in France. During this period she was, therefore, treated as an honoured if unwilling guest in the various country houses where she lived under the indulgent eye of the earl of Shrewsbury. Sensing little danger, Elizabeth permitted Mary to keep her own servants, ride in country parks, and occasionally to visit the baths at Buxton where she met Burghley in 1575 and Leicester in 1578 and 1584. In 1582 Elizabeth once again opened talks to devise conditions for Mary's release and return to Scotland; had the sixteen-year-old James VI of Scotland proved willing to share power with his mother, a deal might well have been done.

In September 1578 Elizabeth reached the age of forty-five. Generally her health was good. Although during the previous year she had been troubled with a leg ulcer – the renewal of a condition suffered in 1570 – she otherwise remained fit, supple and slim thanks to a life of exercise and abstemiousness in eating and drinking. Her most common complaint was the toothache, possibly because she found it difficult to resist sucking sweets.

Despite her youthfulness, most of Elizabeth's courtiers were surprised to learn in the summer of 1578 that she was again considering marriage. Her choice of husband this time was Francis, duke of Anjou, a prince who was more than twenty years her junior. He and his brother, Henry III of France, had been the queen's suitors earlier in the decade, but Henry's courtship had foundered on the question of religion while Elizabeth had never really viewed Francis (then called the duke of Alençon) as a suitable consort before 1578. By contrast the second courtship with Francis was a serious affair and dominated English political life over the next couple of years.

Elizabeth embarked on the Anjou matrimonial negotiations in 1578 as a way to deal with the diplomatic difficulties that were arising from the 'Revolt of the Netherlands'. In 1572 Holland and Zeeland had begun their fight against Spanish rule, and this revolt spread in the mid-1570s to the other fifteen provinces

Despite her youthfulness, most of Elizabeth's courtiers were surprised to learn in the summer of 1578 that she was again considering marriage. Her choice of husband this time was Francis, duke of Anjou, a prince who was more than twenty years her junior.

of the Netherlands. In early 1578, the rebels suffered a major military reverse and it seemed that the Spanish authorities would soon regain total control over their territory unless the rebels received assistance from abroad. Because the rebel leaders were Protestants, fighting in part for freedom of conscience, Elizabeth and her advisers were sympathetic to their struggle. They also recognised that it was in England's strategic interest to prevent Philip II's army from imposing military rule on the region. Nonetheless, unlike many of her advisers, Elizabeth was extremely nervous about sending the rebels military aid for fear of being drawn into a war against Spain, the most powerful state in Europe. As a result of her hesitations, some of the rebel leaders were turning to France for support, and the duke of Anjou, despite his Catholicism, was keen to get involved. His intervention, however, was unwelcome to the English government. Elizabeth and the council were suspicious of his motives and feared that he might demand territory as a reward for his services. What was Elizabeth to do in these circumstances? One suggestion put to her was that she should negotiate a matrimonial treaty with Anjou in the hope that the offer of an English crown might entice him away from pursuing his ambition to be a military hero in the Netherlands.

Initially, few believed that Elizabeth intended ever to go ahead with a marriage to Anjou. They were forced to think again in early 1579 when the duke's trusted household servant, Jean de Simier, visited England. During Simier's stay Elizabeth presented herself as a woman ready for a love-match: she held lengthy interviews with him, where the talk was of love rather than politics; she gave him expensive gifts as love-tokens for the duke; and she found him a pet-name as she was wont to do with all her intimates (in his case he became her monkey or ape as a pun on his name). Her enjoyment of Simier's company and

displays of coquetry were so marked that many believed that she was swept off
her feet as much by the Frenchman's charm and 'courtly dalliances' as by the
thought of marriage to his master. But no matter how much Elizabeth enjoyed
the fun of flirtation, her central concern remained the political advantages of the
match. By 1579 the Anjou project had become the keystone of her foreign policy.
In her opinion, the marriage was necessary not only to counter the menace of
independent French action in the Netherlands but also to cement a dynastic
alliance with Anjou's brother, the king of France, and thereby to end England's
dangerous isolation in Europe. In order to convince the French that she was
genuinely committed to wedding the duke, she had to play the courtship game
as intently and ostentatiously as she could. After all, she had pulled out of so
many matrimonial negotiations in the past that she had acquired a reputation
for insincerity.

Elizabeth's tactics worked well and in August 1579 Anjou came to London
to woo the queen. Although his visit was officially supposed to be secret,
his presence was known to many at court, including the Spanish ambassador.
Elizabeth found her suitor so gallant and attentive that she was neither repulsed
by his pock-marked complexion nor concerned about the age difference
between them. On the contrary she appeared smitten with her 'frog', as she
dubbed him, and during his visit and beyond she played the role of a woman in
love, carrying around his portrait in her prayer-book and writing him a poetic
lament on his departure. At the same time, she evidently thought she could
manipulate the young duke: he would, she believed, probably convert to
Protestantism after their marriage as well as follow her directions if he went
to fight in the Netherlands.

Elizabeth's enthusiasm for Anjou was not shared by the vast majority of her

Amongst the many expressions of hostility to the Anjou match was John Stubbs's pamphlet *The Discoverie of a Gaping Gulf*, which vehemently attacked the French royal family and their religion. To punish him for this offence, Elizabeth ordered that Stubbs should have his hand chopped off.

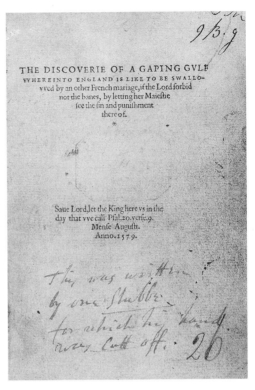

subjects. They hated him for being French, a Catholic, and the son of Catherine de Medici who was widely believed to have ordered the infamous St Bartholomew's Massacre of French Protestants in 1572. During 1579 pamphlets, popular ballads and satirical lampoons were circulated against the match while preachers denounced it in their sermons. Much of the opposition was orchestrated by members of the court and council, particularly those who wanted Elizabeth to make a political alliance with Protestants rather than Catholic rulers. For once in her life, Elizabeth was curiously out of tune with public opinion. Because of her own enthusiasm for the match and her conviction that a royal marriage was no business of the wider public, she was taken completely by surprise at the outburst of hostility. Furthermore, she made little attempt to win round her subjects but instead risked unpopularity by trying to suppress dissent. When John Stubbs had his hand chopped off with a cleaver for daring to write a pamphlet attacking the match, the crowd watched silently in horror.

More seriously for Elizabeth, the council was divided over the match. Its opponents led by Leicester had a long list of objections running from the duke's religion and the risk of childbirth for a middle-aged queen to the threat to England's political independence if Elizabeth bore a son who might inherit the French throne. The opponents of the match lost some momentum when Leicester's secret marriage to Lettice, the widowed countess of Essex, was revealed to the queen. Not only did the earl lose influence with Elizabeth as a consequence of his deceit, but Elizabeth also seemed readier to marry Anjou, as if on the rebound from Leicester. The opponents of the matrimonial scheme, however, recovered the initiative in the council debates of October 1579. Even with one of their number absent, the council divided with seven against the marriage and five, including Burghley, supporting it. Elizabeth was therefore told in so many words that the council could make no recommendation but that she would have to make the decision herself. Elizabeth's response was astounding: she burst into tears. Frustration with her council who had urged her to marry on so many other occasions may be enough to account for her emotional reaction, but some historians believe that she was also genuinely unhappy at having this last chance of marriage and motherhood denied her.

Elizabeth soon recovered her composure, although she remained angry with Leicester, Knollys, Sir Francis Walsingham, and Sir Christopher Hatton, the leading opponents of the match, for some time yet. Nonetheless, her political instincts persuaded her that marriage to the duke was impossible unless she proved able to turn around public opinion and convince her councillors that the advantages of the match outweighed its dangers. This she was clearly unable to do, and the Anjou match was held in abeyance for eighteen months. When in April 1581 a French embassy eventually arrived in England to reactivate the marriage, Elizabeth admitted that she could not sign a matrimonial contract as her subjects still disliked the match. She offered the French king a political treaty instead, but he declined.

The Anjou match had one last breath of life when the duke returned to England in November 1581. On 22 November, Elizabeth declared in front of the court that she would marry Anjou, kissed him on the mouth and gave him her ring. A storm of protest immediately broke out at court and she was forced to retract her promise the next day. Although the early seventeenth-century historian, William Camden, suggested that Elizabeth was carried away by 'the force of modest love in the midst of amorous discourse', it seems more likely that she was hoping to bounce her courtiers into accepting the marriage. She knew that without it she would be unable to obtain the defensive alliance with France, which she desperately wanted to protect her realm against the might of Spain. Thereafter, there was no talk of marriage with Anjou or anyone else. Elizabeth carried on correspondence with her 'dearest' until his death in 1584; she then wore black in mourning and wrote to his mother that she could 'find no consolation except death' which she hoped would reunite them.

The Anjou courtship does not show Elizabeth at her best. Throughout 1579 she showed poor judgement, totally underestimating the anti-Catholic sentiment at court and in London. Furthermore, she was wrong to imagine that Anjou was a pliant pawn; rather he was a loose cannon, as his later military adventures in the Netherlands were amply to demonstrate. It is also doubtful whether the prize of a defensive treaty with France was actually worth having, since that country was on the brink of civil war and no match for Spain. Finally, by focusing on the marriage, Elizabeth postponed making other decisions relating to foreign policy, thereby paralysing the government at a time of great uncertainty and peril.

Changes in the international climate made the danger from Mary Stewart and her Catholic supporters appear more acute to Elizabeth's councillors in the early and mid-1580s. By that time Spanish power had so alarmed the queen that she abandoned appeasement and authorised aggressive measures against Philip II. In 1581 she helped pay for a military expedition in the Netherlands under the command of Anjou. The same year she showed her support for the piratical activities of Francis Drake by knighting him on his return from a voyage around the world during which he had plundered massive amounts of Spanish goods and treasure. Three years later, she signed a treaty offering military assistance to the Dutch provinces still in rebellion against Spain. Understandably Elizabeth's advisers feared Spanish retaliation in the form of a Catholic plot against the queen's life as a preliminary to a full-blown invasion of England. At the same time, the steady trickle of Jesuits illegally entering England after 1580 roused concerns about national security, since these English priests were perceived as seditious conspirators and political agents of both the pope and Spanish king, all of whom would stop at nothing to combat heresy.

Guarding the queen was difficult because of her careless approach to personal safety. Despite warnings, she continued to walk in public, ride on horseback, and travel in open carriages and barges. She refused to restrict right of access to court; and when on progress she accepted gifts, spoke to strangers, and sometimes consumed food and drink before waiting for tasters to test for poison. She was at least as vulnerable to assassination attempts as William of Orange, the Protestant leader of the Dutch rebels, who was murdered by his Catholic serving-man in 1584. Her safety, therefore, depended heavily on the intelligence gathering carried out by a spy network under the supervision of Sir Francis Walsingham, her principal secretary since December 1573. Thanks to his dedication and the efficiency of his agents, two major plots were detected in the mid-1580s: the Throckmorton Plot of 1583 and Parry Plot of 1584.

There can be little doubt that the Throckmorton Plot was a genuinely dangerous conspiracy involving amongst others Mary Stewart's French relations, the Spanish ambassador Bernardino de Mendoza, Jesuit priests, and an English Catholic gentleman named Francis Throckmorton. On the other hand, the Parry

Plot was a more murky affair and it is still difficult to determine whether its instigator, Dr William Parry, was really a potential assassin or rather a government agent playing the role of agent provocateur amongst Catholics. Whatever the truth, the timing of both these plots during years of intense international tension made the government extremely nervous about Mary, who was viewed as the focus if not the fomenter of Catholic conspiracy. She was therefore moved to more secure castles – first Tutbury and then Chartley in Staffordshire – under the much stricter surveillance of Sir Amias Paulet, a zealous Protestant who had no time for Mary's royal pretensions and treated his charge as a dangerous political prisoner.

After the exposure of the Throckmorton and Parry Plots, both Burghley and Walsingham took the lead in thinking up new ways to protect Elizabeth. It was probably Burghley who dreamed up the so-called Bond of Association, a kind of voluntary brotherhood of loyal gentlemen, which was designed to defend Elizabeth's life and stop Mary reaping any benefit from a successful assassination attempt on her. Signatories to the Bond first swore to pursue anyone who attempted to harm the queen 'to the utter extermination of them, their counsellors, aiders and abettors'. In a second clause they then bound themselves to bar from the succession any person 'by whom and for whom any such detestable act shall be attempted', and they promised 'to prosecute such person

Opposite: This manuscript is the first page
of a prayer drawn up after the discovery
of the Parry Plot. Thanks are offered to
God for establishing Elizabeth on the
throne and delivering her (and England)
from her enemies.
The British Library, Lansdowne MS 116, f.77

or persons to death'. In this way, it was hoped, the Bond would deter Mary's supporters from entering into conspiracies either with or without her knowledge. Copies of the Bond were sent to counties and towns all over England, and thousands signed it to display their loyalty to the queen.

In November 1584, attempts were made to convert the Bond into an act of parliament 'for the surety of the queen's most royal person'. Elizabeth, who had probably been ambivalent about the wording of the original Bond, now intervened to announce her objections to the legislation. Her main complaint was that a form of lynch-law might be used against an anointed sovereign, but she was also concerned about the succession since the wording of the oath was so ambiguous that it could result in the exclusion of James VI as well as his mother. Elizabeth, therefore, made known to parliament that she 'would not consent that anyone should be punished for the fault of another'. She demanded that there be proof of Mary's complicity in a plot before punishment was meted out, and required that James VI should not be included within the compass of the act unless he were directly involved in treason. The final version of the statute reflected her concerns and input.

Even more so than Burghley, Walsingham was convinced that Elizabeth could never be safe while the 'bosom serpent', as he called Mary, remained alive. He therefore developed a plan to entrap Mary in a plot that would justify her execution by the terms of the 1584 statute. By using a double agent, Gilbert Gifford, Walsingham ensured that Mary communicated secretly with her supporters via notes concealed in false bottoms of beer barrels. Through his assistant, the brilliant code-breaker Thomas Phelippes, all Mary's correspondence was deciphered and copied before being smuggled in and out of Mary's residence at Chartley in the barrels. By this means Walsingham discovered the details of a

O Eternal God and mercifull father, wee thie vnworthie
Creatures, most humblie doe confesse, that wee ar not hable
with owre tongues to vtter, nor in owre hartes to conceaue
the exceading measure of thine infinite goodnes, graces, and
fauours in this later age shewed to this Noble Realme, in
that thow (O Lord) hast in most dangerous times, a few
yeres past, by thy goodnes and prouidence beyond expectation of man, directed and preserued the tender
and noble parson of owre noble Soueraigne Lady
Elizabeth, by thy grace, according to hir right, to
cum to this kingdome and Roiall seate of hir noble
father, and by hir, being thearein stablished, as thy
deare beloued chosen servant, to deliuer vs thy people
that weare as Captiues to Babilon, owt of Bondage,
and thraldome of the Enemies of thy trewe Churche
and to restore vs againe to thee free fruition of the
Gospell of thy Sonne owre Sauio Christ, for the enioy-
eng wherof now these manie yeres, wee doe confesse and acknowledge
that beyond all owre desartes, yea trewly o Lord, what
wee by owre daily vnthankefulnes for the benefitt of thy
Gospell, and by owre sinfull liues, contrarie to owre bold
profession, haue most iustlie prouoked thee to withdrawe
thy fauo from vs, thow O Lord, with thy mercifull fauour
and mightie power did strengthend thy good blessed servant owre most gratious Quene, constantly agaimst the

plot to murder Elizabeth, rescue Mary, and raise a Catholic rising at home. The plotters were a mixture of Catholic priests, madcap adventurers and respectable gentlemen. It was one of the latter – Anthony Babington – who sent Mary an outline of the plan to keep her informed and seek her approval. Her reply on 18 July 1586 provided Walsingham with the evidence he needed of Mary's complicity. Phelippes copied the letter and sent it to Walsingham with a small picture of a gallows on its seal.

When she learned of the plot, Elizabeth was determined to make a terrible example of Babington and his fellow conspirators. She ordered that they should die as painfully as possible, namely that they should be disembowelled and mutilated (drawn and quartered) before they had died at the end of a rope. But after seven of them were executed in this way and the details of their suffering had been conveyed to the queen, together with a note that the crowd had registered its cruelty, she changed her instructions. The following day the second batch of condemned men was 'hung till they were quite dead before they were cut down and boweled'.

Elizabeth felt betrayed by Mary's approval of the plot to assassinate her. Calling Mary a 'wicked murderess', she condemned 'her treacherous dealings' towards the one person who had been 'the saviour of her life for many a year'. Nonetheless Elizabeth did not embrace the opportunity to destroy her enemy with any kind of energy or enthusiasm. On the contrary she dragged her feet at every stage of the proceedings that led to Mary's trial, condemnation and execution, and she tried to disassociate herself from the course of events that was leading inexorably to Mary's death. She would not have Mary brought down to the Tower but had her put on trial in the castle of Fotheringhay in Northamptonshire. There the trial commissioners – a group of thirty-six peers,

This drawing shows three different stages of the execution of Mary Queen of Scots in the great hall at Fotheringhay Castle: first Mary's arrival; then her disrobing on the scaffold; and finally the executioner ready to strike at her head on the block.
The British Library, Add. MS 48027, f.650

judges and councillors – were not allowed to deliver their verdict. Although she shortly afterwards agreed to them delivering a judgement at Westminster, she delayed until December the signing of the proclamation which announced the death sentence against Mary. Knowing that parliament would call for Mary's immediate execution, as it had in 1572, she tried to avoid summoning a new session and only caved in when confronted with concerted pressure from her councillors. When parliament met on 29 October 1586 she did not attend its opening; two weeks later she accepted its petition requesting the immediate execution of Mary but asked them to think again. When the members came up with the same advice, she explained to them her quandary and asked them to 'excuse my doubtfulness, and take in good part my answer-answerless'.

What troubled Elizabeth was horror at the prospect of authorising the public execution of a kinswoman and anointed queen. She never accepted the arguments of her councillors that Mary had lost her royal status upon entering England, but felt that regicide would be a blemish on her own honour and a worrying precedent for the future. Events were to prove her right on both counts. At the same time, however, Elizabeth felt little, if any, tenderness or sentimentality towards Mary herself and was content to see her die – just not publicly by her authority. On one occasion she hinted to members of her parliament that private individuals should take the law into their own hands according to the provisions of the Bond of Association. Later, she intimated to Paulet that he should quietly end the life of his prisoner. Conveniently forgetting that he had signed the Bond the previous year, Paulet robustly rejected any such suggestion: 'God forbid that I should make so foul a shipwreck of my conscience'.

It was only after another plot against Elizabeth's life was opportunely revealed in early 1587 that Elizabeth decided to sign the death warrant. On 1 February she handed over the signed copy to William Davison, her recently appointed junior secretary of state, and on 8 February Mary was executed at Fotheringhay. When Elizabeth heard the news she was overwhelmed with grief and anger. Her grief at what she considered a sacrilegious deed was probably genuine; her anger at the warrant's dispatch without her express consent, if not feigned, was certainly unjustified, although it probably stemmed from a more general wrath at her councillors' hard-line position throughout the crisis. Davison bore the brunt of her fury and was sent to the Tower for eighteen months, but Burghley did not escape scot-free for she refused to receive his letters or allow him into her presence for weeks after the execution. As late as June she was still 'calling him traitor, false dissembler and wicked wretch'. When Elizabeth at last calmed down, she attempted a damage-limitation exercise, which was needed because Mary's death had been greeted with fury in Paris and Edinburgh. Mary was buried with full honours at Peterborough Cathedral in July 1587 at Elizabeth's expense.

In general, historians have been critical of Elizabeth's treatment of the Scottish queen. Early writers like the late-seventeenth-century Edmund Bohun

accused Elizabeth of acting out of revenge and jealousy, and denounced Mary's
trial and execution as 'a detestable piece of wickedness'. Historians today, on the
other hand, tend to accept that the execution was necessary but condemn
Elizabeth for her indecisiveness. In truth Elizabeth was placed between a rock
and a hard place, and no-one would help her out. Mary had behaved foolishly,
showing she could not be trusted; the Scots refused her restoration; while the
English council and parliament were implacable in their demands for Mary's
death. These circumstances forced Elizabeth into taking a decision which she felt
was morally wrong and knew would damage her reputation eternally. No wonder
she prevaricated and then tried to place the blame elsewhere.

Elizabeth thought of herself as a providential ruler, God's instrument for restoring
the Gospel to England after the Roman captivity of the Church under Mary I.
In her private and public prayers she identified herself with the prophet Daniel,
comparing his deliverance from the lions' den to her own release from the Tower
of London and Woodstock. Elizabeth's Protestant subjects also liked to portray
her as a providential ruler, although they preferred to compare her to Deborah,
Judith, David, and Solomon, biblical figures who had triumphed over their pagan
neighbours and cleansed Israel of idolatry. In this way they hoped to persuade the
queen that her divine mission was to take up arms against Catholics at home and
abroad, and purge the realm of all traces of popery.

Sincere Protestant though she was, Elizabeth's religious tastes embraced
conservative elements much disliked by those Protestants who had been
influenced by the teachings of 'reformed' theologians such as John Calvin. Her
love of ceremony and ritual has already been mentioned, as has its influence on
the 1559 religious settlement, but we should also note her predilection for private

prayer over edifying sermons, her respect for the Virgin Mary, her insistence on retaining a silver cross and candlesticks in her royal chapel, her unwillingness to abstain from all sports and pleasure on the Sabbath, and her readiness to deliver oaths which most zealous Protestants found blasphemous ('God's death' was one of her favourites). All these preferences marked Elizabeth out as different from strict Calvinists who tried to follow precisely the precepts and principles laid down in the scriptures. For them Elizabeth did not come close to the model of the godly rulers in the Hebrew Bible whom they wanted her to emulate.

When these Protestants likened Elizabeth to biblical heroes in their attempts to exhort her to complete the work of godly reform, their eulogies were less a form of flattery than of prescription. As one preacher allegedly explained, 'he had no other way to instruct the queen what she should be, but by commending her'. Sometimes, though, preachers adopted a different tone and rebuked her in sermons for her shortcomings. On these occasions, Elizabeth usually sat silently in her closet in the chapel but there were moments when she could not resist delivering an angry retort. Recognising Alexander Nowell's allusion to her silver cross and candlesticks in his sermon on Ash Wednesday 1565, she reportedly interrupted him with the words: 'Leave that, it has nothing to do with your subject and the matter is now threadbare'. When criticism slipped into impertinence or confrontation Elizabeth showed her displeasure forcefully, as Edward Dering found to his cost after delivering a sermon that accused the queen of neglecting her Church.

Although Elizabeth could not silence her Protestant critics, she was determined to stop them mounting a challenge to her vision of the Church. Members of parliament who tried to enact religious reforms were a particular irritant to her, and she repeatedly insisted that they had no right to introduce such legislation on their own initiative, even when the bills had the backing of bishops or councillors. When some brave members ignored her warnings and went ahead with their own radical legislative programme to change the form of liturgy in the Church, she had a few of them arrested and ensured that their proposals never became law. Elizabeth was equally insistent that her Protestant clergy could not slide out of observing existing legal requirements. Her demand for complete conformity sprang in part from a deep-seated political conservatism that revered royal authority, law and order, but it also arose from a strong fear of 'novelty' and 'diversity' in religion. To her mind they were a poison that would disturb, if not destroy, 'Christian charity, unity and concord'.

It was fear of 'new-fangledness', disorder and divisiveness that prompted Elizabeth in 1576 to require an end to prophesyings, an order that brought her into direct confrontation with Edmund Grindal, her second archbishop of Canterbury. Prophesyings, which were regional meetings where local clergy and lay people would hear preaching and scriptural exegesis, were liked by most bishops as both an essential aid for training preachers and a way of spreading the Word. Elizabeth, on the other hand, was suspicious of these religious exercises, because she had heard that they provided radical and nonconforming clergy with a platform to teach and defend unorthodox and dangerous opinions. Although Grindal was prepared to regulate prophesyings more closely, he refused point blank to suppress them. In a 6,000-word letter written on 8 December 1576 to the queen, he explained that he preferred 'to offend your earthly majesty than to offend against the heavenly majesty of God'. In the same document he exhorted Elizabeth to follow the example of Christian Roman emperors in the past and listen to the bishops: 'Who can deny', he wrote, 'that in cases of faith bishops were wont to judge emperors and not emperors of bishops?' For this affront and his refusal to apologise or make a retraction, Elizabeth confined Grindal to his official residence and suspended him from his duties for six months. She would have dismissed him from his office, had not Burghley, Walsingham and other councillors persuaded her to be more lenient. Grindal continued as archbishop until his death in 1583, carrying out routine administrative duties but was denied any active role in the government of the Church.

Elizabeth's next archbishop was far more to her liking, and she nicknamed him her 'little black husband'. John Whitgift had been a well-known opponent of nonconformity even before his appointment to Canterbury; once *in situ*, he immediately began with Elizabeth's backing to impose the 1559 prayer book on all the clergy and stamp out radical dissent. As a result of his efforts, nonconforming clergy lost their livings and licenses to preach; outspoken Presbyterians (those who wanted the abolition of bishops) were prosecuted and imprisoned; and two radical sectarians lost their lives. Thanks to Whitgift's energy, Elizabeth emerged as the victor in her battle with Protestant nonconformity, but it was at the cost of creating a small group of alienated godly people who were nicknamed 'puritans' by their enemies.

While Elizabeth's religious conservatism frustrated so many 'godly' Protestants and prevented the structural reform of the Church, it did much to make England a place of relative religious peace. The prayer book she endorsed was generally inclusive, as it stressed Christian fundamentals rather than divisive doctrines, and in time it came to be popular with church congregations. Puritan practices on the other hand antagonised many parishioners who were attached to traditional rites, disliked long sermons, and had no wish to abandon fun on a Sunday. Had she imposed the puritans' version of true religion, instead of her own, on all her subjects, there might well have been serious political unrest in England.

She knew the value of propaganda,
and through her ministers she
encouraged writers to defend the
regime and answer Catholic attacks
on its religion and policies.

Triumphs and decline

Criticised though she was for her religious and political policies, Elizabeth usually
proved adept at public relations. She knew the value of propaganda, and through
her ministers she encouraged writers to defend the regime and answer Catholic
attacks on its religion and policies. As the reign progressed, moreover, she
approved measures to tighten up censorship against prose writings and plays
deemed subversive. Shakespeare was just one of many playwrights to fall foul of
the master of the revels, the official censor of drama, and he had to accept the
removal of the deposition scene from *Richard II*, references to Ireland in *Henry V*,
and passages dealing with rebel grievances in *Henry IV*. Elizabeth probably would
have liked an equally strong control over the production of her portrait, but in
practice she could only encourage the use of authorised face patterns, and her
council had at times to resort to ordering the destruction of 'unseemly' pictures
on sale in the street.

Elizabeth understood well that her strength as a ruler depended quite
heavily on outward appearances. Consequently, she took great pains to present
herself as a majestic monarch, wearing clothes cut in the latest styles, made of
the richest fabrics, and adorned with large and precious gems. The effect was
sometimes dazzling. One foreign nobleman who visited England in the mid-
1580s commented that 'the queen, while sitting alone in the ornamental carriage,
looked like goddesses are wont to be painted'; another visitor from abroad
described her in the late 1590s as 'glittering with the glory of majesty'. She liked
to wear black and white, and often courtiers also wore these colours to display
their allegiance.

Although Elizabeth insisted on strict formality at court, she never remained
aloof but instead conversed with guests in a dignified yet relaxed manner and
singled out for attention individuals who were standing in the crowd gathered

Previous page: The 'Ditchley Portrait' (c. 1592), by Marcus Gheeraerts the Younger, which depicts Elizabeth in the heavens, symbolically banishing the storms behind her. Her feet, however, are firmly planted on the globe at the manor of Ditchley in Oxfordshire, the home of Sir Henry Lee who commissioned the painting.
National Portrait Gallery

Below: George Gascoigne presents Elizabeth with his poetic drama, the *Hermit's Tale*, which was performed for her at Woodstock in Oxfordshire in 1575. *The British Library, Royal MS 18 A XLVIII, f.1*

Opposite: One of the many lavish entertainments held for Elizabeth. This picture depicts Elvetham in Hampshire. *The British Library, 193 a13 Vol II*

about her. One foreign diarist described how she spoke 'very graciously, first to one, then to another', while she processed through her court towards chapel on a Sunday. On another occasion, the Spanish ambassador noticed that during her progress she 'ordered her carriage to be taken sometimes where the crowd seemed thickest and stood up and thanked the people' for their joyful reception of her. She also made a point of putting at ease inexperienced dignitaries who had been given the honour of delivering before her a speech of welcome, as when she told a nervous schoolteacher who had to address her in Latin, 'Be not afraid'. In this respect, she resembled Diana, the late princess of Wales: both women were so glamorous in appearance that they inspired awe, yet both could put aside formality and relate directly to adoring members of a crowd.

Elizabeth was most accessible to the residents of London. They could see her when she moved between the royal palaces of Richmond, Hampton Court, Whitehall and Greenwich or attended traditional royal spectacles such as the annual procession of the Knights of the Garter on St George's Day, or the less frequent opening of the houses of parliament. Large numbers could also glimpse her as they watched the tournaments held later in the reign at Whitehall to celebrate her Accession Day. With the help of Sir Henry Lee (master of the

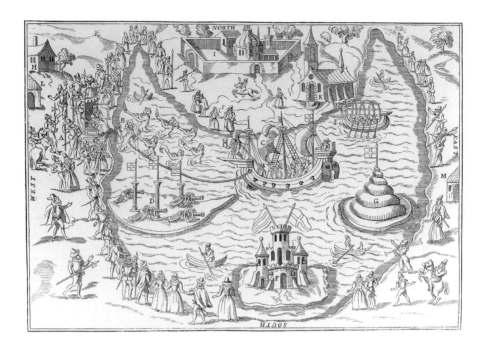

armoury), Elizabeth made these latter festivities as theatrical, colourful and regal as possible in order to enhance the prestige of the monarchy. For the same purpose, she also kept on ancient ceremonies associated with sacral monarchy which Protestant reformers had condemned as superstitious. On Maundy Thursday she washed the feet of poor women (the number corresponded to the years in the queen's age) while at Easter and on summer progresses she carried out the royal touch in order to cure magically the disease of scrofula, known as the king's evil (a form of tuberculosis in the neck).

The opportunity for non-Londoners to see Elizabeth came during progresses held during the summer months. Although she never went further north than Stafford nor beyond Bristol to the south-west, she toured much of southern England and visited corporate towns as well as the estates of her nobility and gentlemen. During the first half of the reign, these progresses were an annual occurrence, but after 1580 the queen rarely travelled further afield than her royal palaces along the Thames. She set off again on provincial progress only in 1591 and 1592 and then between 1599 and 1602. These journeys through the shires not only allowed the queen to show herself to her subjects but they also were occasions when the most important of them could impress her with their

+ Copy of her Ma:ties most gracious Answer deliuered by hir self
personally to the Petitions of the L̃ and Commons of his
weekly Parliament. the 12 of 9bre 1586

[_]ottomles graces and immeasurable benefitts bestowed vpon mee by Almightie God
and haue bin such, as I must not only acknowledg them but also admire them, accoun-
ting them as well miracles, as benefitts, not so much in respect of his diuine Ma:tie
with whome nothing is more common then to do thinges rare & singuler as in regard
of oure weaknes, who cannot sufficiently set forth his wonderfull woorkes & graces
w:ch to mee wont haue bene so many, so diuerslie folded and imbrodered one vpon
another as in no sort I am able to expresse them.

And although there liueth not any that may more iustly acknowledg them selues
infinitely bounde vnto God then I may, whose life he hath wonderfully preserued
at sondrie tymes (beyond my merit) frome a multitude of perills and daungers.
Yet is not that the thing for w:ch I account my self deepliest bound to giue him the
most hartie thanckes, or to yeld him the greatest recognition, but this w:ch I shall
tell you hereafter, w:ch will deserue the name of wonder. If rare things and
some seene be worthie for accompted, namely that as I came to the Crowne
with the willing hartes of my subiects so do I now after xxviij yeres raigne
perceaue in you all no deminution of your goodwilles, w:ch if happelie I
should wante, well mowght I breath, but not thincke I liued, if that were
diminished.

ALSO now notwithstanding if I finde apparantlie my life hath bin full daungero:slie
rouslie sought, and my death by her contriued. Yet am I in respect thereof so cleare
frome malice, which hath the propertie to make men gladde, and reuie:fill at y:e
falls and faultes of theire enemies, and make them seeme to do thinges for other
cawses, when as with ranco: they are stirred to pursue theire intentions: I
pirates it is to mee, and hath bene a thing most grieuous to thincke that one
not different in sex, of like estate, and my neare kinne, shold be so woorse of grace
or false in faith as now to seeke my death, by whome so long her life hath bene
preserued w:ch th' intollerable perill of my owne: yea I had so litle purpose
to pursue her with any coloure of malice, y:t as it is not vnknowne to some of my
LL: here (for now I will play the blabb) I secretlie wrote her a l:re vpon the
discouerie of treasons, that if she wolde confesse them thoroughlie of hir owne course
confesse it and priuatlie acknowledge it by her l:res vnto mee, shee neuer should be
called for it into publike question. Neither did I it of any minde to circumuent her,
for then I knew as much as shee cold confesse and so did I write.

ALSO now the matter is made so apparant, I thought shee trulie
were repentant (as perhapps she wolde easely appeare in wittig sheowe) and that
for her none other wolde take the matter vppon them, or that we were but as two
milke maides, w:th pailes vpon oure armes, or that there were no more dependency
vpon us, but myne owne life were onlie in perill, and not the whole estate
of youre religion and well doings, I protest (wherein you may beleeue mee, for
although I may haue many vices, I hope I haue not accustomed my tongue
to be an instrument of vntruthe) I wolde most willinglie pardon and remit
this offence.

speeches, hospitality, and entertainment. During the 1570s, the hospitality offered became more lavish, and Elizabeth's hosts commissioned well-known poets of the day to write elaborate pageants, masques, and pastimes to amuse her. These dramatic productions usually conjured up an idealised world of pastoral bliss, which drew upon themes from mythology and chivalric romance. They frequently included the queen as a participant in the drama, and invariably eulogised her. A political or personal agenda nearly always lay behind the panegyric. When Elizabeth visited Leicester's estates at Kenilworth Castle in July 1575, for example, he put on a number of outdoor entertainments, which were designed to promote both his matrimonial suit and the political programme of militant Protestantism he sponsored on the council. Accounts of the progresses were often printed in pamphlets both as propaganda for the queen and publicity for the poets and their patrons.

Elizabeth's speeches (or at least the most important ones) were also printed and circulated for propaganda purposes. Unlike Mary Tudor and Mary Stewart, Elizabeth presumed to take on the masculine role of delivering public addresses in English or Latin to ambassadors, parliament, and the universities. The content of these orations, which the queen composed, probably had a public appeal, as they emphasised values shared amongst the educated elite: patriotism, loyalty, obedience, a respect for precedent, and a reverence for religion and classical wisdom. They also demonstrated the rhetorical skills much admired by educated

Elizabethans. Some speeches, such as the one delivered at Tilbury in 1588, employed a 'Senecan' type of rhetoric – direct, concise, structured, and rhythmic – and had an appeal that can still be appreciated today. Others, which followed a 'Ciceronian' model, were complex in construction, ambiguous, and oblique, qualities which, though respected during the Renaissance, make their meaning baffling to a modern reader.

There is strong evidence that listeners were very proud of their queen's eloquence. Her dramatic delivery and mastery of the classical rhetorical style were impressive, especially as she did not read out her speeches from a set text but delivered them more or less impromptu; most of the manuscript copies that exist today were written down afterwards from memory or notes. After she had publicly rebuked a Polish diplomat in 1597, Robert Cecil recounted the incident to the earl of Essex, writing 'her Majesty made one of the best answers *ex tempore* in Latin that ever I heard', and manuscript copies of the oration were circulated fairly widely to show off her skill. In 1601, a listener who was trying to note one of her speeches commented that 'the grace of pronunciation and of her apt and refined words, so learnedly composed, did ravish the sense of the hearers with such admiration as every new sentence made me half forget the precedents'. Perhaps Elizabeth dazzled these men because women did not normally perform on the public stage. Nonetheless, both during her lifetime and afterwards, Elizabeth's eloquence and talent for self-presentation marked her out as an exceptional monarch.

During the first twenty years of her reign Elizabeth had been depicted in poetry, pageantry and portraits as a chaste but marriageable queen. After 1578, however, she began to be celebrated as a Virgin Queen, and England's power became symbolically associated with her celibacy and unmarried status. This new

departure started during the period of the Anjou courtship when opponents of
the French match commissioned or executed art and literary works idealising
Elizabeth's virginity as part of their publicity campaign against the matrimonial
project. Once it became clear that the match would not go ahead and that
Elizabeth would die unwed, both she and her courtiers saw advantages in lauding
her life-long virginity in poetry and portraits. The breakdown of relations
with Spain was another powerful drive for the development of Elizabeth's
identification with the virginal Classical goddesses Diana, Cynthia, Astraea and
Venus-Virgo. During the lengthy period when foreign invasion was feared,
Elizabeth's natural and virginal body worked well as a metaphor for the
impregnability of the body politic or state against foreign attack.

Before 1585 Elizabeth had hoped a war against Spain could be avoided,
mainly because she feared the superiority of Philip II's armed forces. Nevertheless, as international tension between the two countries intensified during the
1570s, she prepared for the worst and earmarked considerable sums of money for

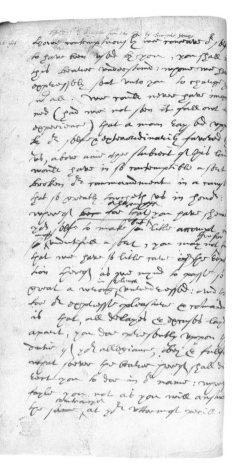

the modernisation of England's navy. The number of ships increased and their design was improved so that they had better manoeuvrability and more effective gun-power. Hostilities against Spain did not begin with any formal declaration of war, but with two acts of aggression ordered by the queen. In late 1585, she sent a small army to fight in the Netherlands under the leadership of Leicester, and she dispatched Drake to raid the Caribbean and attack Iberian vessels harboured in Spain. Elizabeth did not intend these military actions to provoke a full-scale war; indeed worries that they might do so caused her to hesitate several times before giving both men their final orders. Her objective was to induce Philip II to call off his military offensive in the Netherlands and sign a permanent peace treaty that would guarantee religious toleration and virtual autonomy for his Dutch subjects. To assist this process, she opened up five simultaneous sets of peace negotiations with Spain between 1585 and 1588. She also refused to accept the Dutch offer of sovereignty of the Netherlands, and was furious when Leicester, acting on his own initiative, accepted the post of governor-general of the Netherlands, which implied an English sovereignty.

Elizabeth's offensives, however, provoked Philip II into mobilising his resources against England. An Armada of 125 vessels set out from Spain in 1588. The plan was for it to arrive at a fixed point in the Channel, from where it could

Previous page: This drawing (c. 1576) is probably the earliest visual representation of Elizabeth as the Virgin Queen. It forms the frontispiece of a Latin eulogy written by the closet Catholic Lord Henry Howard in a bid to secure royal favour.
The British Library, Egerton MS 944, f.1v

Opposite: The defeat of the Spanish Armada, in an engraving by the Elizabethan cartographer Robert Adams, showing the dramatic engagement of both fleets.
The British Library, G 929

act as a bodyguard escorting barges containing some 17,000 foreign soldiers from Flanders to Kent, before landing itself. Had the invasion force landed, it is difficult to see how Elizabeth's makeshift army could have resisted such an experienced and disciplined force. But the Spanish strategy depended upon good weather, exact timing, and excellent communications between the leader of the Spanish army stationed in Dunkirk and the commander of the Armada fleet, vital ingredients which were lacking once the invasion was set in motion.

In July 1588 the Armada was sighted off the Cornish coast. Despite efforts of the English navy to stop its progress, it continued on its way towards its rendezvous with the army of Flanders off Calais. While it was anchored there, English fireships loaded with explosives were released and drifted towards them. In panic the Spanish fleet dispersed, sailing northwards, and the next day the English navy attacked off Gravelines. Few Spanish ships were actually sunk in the battle but the Armada took a battering and the sailors on board became demoralised. Instead of regrouping, the ships scattered, driven by strong winds northwards, and they were forced to return to Spain by circumnavigating the British Isles. On the journey home, storms shipwrecked about a third of the navy and drowned perhaps half of the 30,000 seamen.

The defeat of the Spanish Armada did more than any other event of the reign to enhance Elizabeth's reputation amongst contemporaries and later historians. Both the official propaganda and spontaneous outbursts of relief fully exploited scriptural parallels and compared the Spanish defeat to the drowning of Pharaoh's army in the Red Sea, the slaying by David of Goliath, and Deborah's victory over the Canaanites. English Protestants now had evidence that God was truly on Elizabeth's side, whatever the failings of her religious policy. Sermons, ballads, pamphlets, and commemorative medals celebrated the victory as a miracle

performed by God on behalf of a godly ruler and nation. It was Elizabeth's inspection of her troops at Tilbury on 29 and 30 July 1588 that has particularly captured the imagination of historians. Although no entirely reliable eyewitness account of the visit exists, biographers from the early seventeenth century onwards have manufactured their own descriptions of Elizabeth's appearance and speech at Tilbury. She is usually mounted on a white horse, dressed in armour, and holding a truncheon; she always delivers a resounding oration which fortifies her troops. The familiar sentence, 'I know I have the body but of a weak and feeble woman, but I have the heart and stomach of a king,' was based on the recollections of an eyewitness but did not appear in print until 1654. Earlier manuscript versions of the speech are rather different but expressed similar martial sentiments, drew attention to the weaknesses of her sex, and emphasised the godly nature of the war. For many biographers the Tilbury visit demonstrated Elizabeth's courage and success as a war leader. According to Camden, 'incredible it is how much she strengthened the hearts of her captains and soldiers by her presence and speech', and his view was repeated in countless narratives of the reign.

Below: Portrait of Sir Walter Ralegh, wearing Elizabeth's colours and a pearl in his ear.
National Portrait Gallery

The 'Armada Portrait' (of which there are three extant copies) was one of the many artefacts produced to celebrate England's naval victory over Spain. In this painting, a strong association is made between the virginity of the queen's body and the power of the English state. Bows and pearls, which are symbols of virginity, freely decorate Elizabeth's dress, but one pearl and a tied knot are positioned ostentatiously where a male codpiece would have been. In this way they signify that Elizabeth's potency lay in her virginity. Furthermore, a causal relationship was established between Elizabeth's virginity and England's victory through the device of spatially linking the destruction of the Armada (shown through the windows on each side of the queen) with the lines of her stomacher which meet in a triangular point at the most prominent pearl and bow.

Until the end of the reign, the defeat of the Spanish Armada continued to influence the way that Elizabeth was portrayed in poetry and paintings. In the 'Ditchley Portrait', for example, she is shown as a celestial figure controlling the elements; with her back to a tempest, she ushers in the bright weather that signifies a new golden age. The identification of Elizabeth with the chaste moon goddesses, Diana and Cynthia, likewise, owed a great deal to England's naval

The 'Armada Portrait' by George Gower, which celebrated Elizabeth as a victorious monarch who saved England from the Spanish invasion. Through the window on the left English fireships can be seen attacking the Armada, and on the right the Spanish ships are shown being wrecked in the storms.
Bridgeman Art Library

success in the Spanish War. Initially, the identification had arisen as a private pun
used by Sir Walter Ralegh. As the queen nicknamed Ralegh 'water', the courtier's
frequent references to her in his poetry as the moon goddess who controlled the
tides or waters were intended as a statement about his personal relationship with
his monarch. His portrait of 1588 similarly played on the pun as a clever way to
represent himself as the queen's devoted servant, ready to follow her every whim.
In its top left-hand corner, a small crescent moon (symbolising the queen) was
painted over his motto *Amor et Virtute* (love and virtue) while Ralegh was dressed
in her colours of black and white with a large pearl (her emblem) in his left ear.
Ralegh's courtly conceit, however, soon developed into a more general fashion,
because the moon goddess was an appropriate symbol for Elizabeth's power over
the seas and oceans after the defeat of the Armada and at a time when England's
privateers were inflicting huge damage on Spanish shipping. Furthermore, Diana
as an armed maiden was a perfect image for a female ruler who ruled a country
at war. Consequently in miniatures and paintings, Elizabeth was frequently shown
with the attributes of Diana (most often the crescent moon) while in poetry
and pageants she was addressed as Cynthia, Diana and Phoebe (another name
for the moon).

It would be a mistake to conclude that representations of Elizabeth as
a Virgin Queen implied the adulation of her subjects. In the first place,
representations of her as divine should not be taken literally, for they drew on
literary conventions used in Renaissance Europe with a pedigree that went back
to medieval romance and the poetry of the fourteenth-century poet Petrarch.
Second, the panegyric of much literary work often masked the disillusionment
and dissent of its author; Edmund Spenser's *Fairie Queene*, for example, was a
critique of Elizabeth's rule despite its reputation as a celebration of Gloriana.

It would be a mistake to conclude that representations of Elizabeth as a Virgin Queen implied the adulation of her subjects.

At the same time it is likely that the representations of Elizabeth as an immortal being were disguising anxieties about her death and an uncertain succession; after all, the moon can symbolise continuity through change. Finally, many of the representations of Elizabeth as a virginal goddess were designed to honour the patron commissioning the work at least as much as the queen. While the 'Ditchley Portrait', commissioned by Sir Henry Lee, depicted Elizabeth as the queen of heavens, it also commemorated her visit to Lee's house, for the royal foot was placed on the globe at his estate of Ditchley in Oxfordshire. The 'Procession Portrait', which shows Elizabeth as a virginal figure sitting aloft in a triumphal car, is actually dominated by the figure of the earl of Worcester who was the most likely patron of the painting. For all these reasons, the popular assumption that there was a 'cult of the Virgin Queen' calls for renewed discussion.

After the defeat of the Armada, the war against Spain was somewhat an anticlimax: no pitched battles took place on land or sea, and England won no spectacular victories against Spain. Although a new war front opened up in France in 1589, the English armies dispatched there were small, and the soldiers usually operated as reinforcements in the armies of the French Huguenot leader Henry of Navarre (soon to be crowned Henry IV) against his Catholic enemies. After 1594, Elizabeth began to rein in her continental commitments and resisted the advice of hawks on the council that she continue to fight alongside the French and Dutch until Spain suffered total military collapse. She agreed to several ambitious strikes at sea against Spain after 1588, but they failed in their strategic objectives and most ended in ignominy. Even the English sack of Cadiz in 1596, which was a huge blow to Spanish pride, degenerated into a scramble for spoils and brought little financial reward or long-term benefit to the queen. As a result, Elizabeth gradually lost confidence in the aggressive naval strategy urged by

Previous page: *Eliza Triumphans*, known
as the 'Procession Portrait' (c. 1600–01)
attributed to Robert Peake, shows
Elizabeth sitting aloft in a triumphal
car. Dressed in bright orange and
wearing the Order of the Garter
necklace is Edward Somerset, the fourth
earl of Worcester, who very probably
commissioned the work.
By kind permission of
Mr J. K. Wingfield Digby

her commanders and eventually stopped direct attacks on Spanish territory.
Despite peace talks being opened between the two sides, the war was not
concluded until the next reign.

Elizabeth was under considerable stress during the war years. Her
councillors bombarded her with unwelcome advice, while generals and naval
commanders frequently disobeyed or deliberately misconstrued her instructions.
Money poured out of her coffers yet the war dragged on with no end in sight.
To make matters worse, rebellion erupted in Ireland in 1595 under the resourceful
Hugh O'Neill who called on the Spaniards for aid and launched a major
challenge to English rule. Elizabeth sought escape from these public concerns
by reading the scriptures and translating classical works. According to Camden,
at the time of one setback in 1593, she 'daily turned over Boethius his books
De Consolatio and translated them handsomely into the English tongue'. She also
began to withdraw more often to her privy chamber where she received only
her most intimate friends and councillors.

Elizabeth's running of the Spanish war was severely criticised both then
and now. Accusations of indecisiveness were frequent at the time because she no
sooner issued orders to her military men than she revoked or modified them. She
was also accused of fighting the war with an unseemly parsimony, since she was
niggardly when faced with demands for money and balked at the cost of most
military enterprises. Temperamentally Elizabeth was unsuited to the kind of bold
decision-making and risk-taking strategies associated with great war leaders, while
her natural instinct for financial prudence meant that she was determined to
balance her books. Nevertheless, it needs to be remembered that Elizabeth had
good reason to contain spending on warfare and to think twice before agreeing
to expensive military campaigns. England simply did not have the resources for

ambitious projects. As it was, the eighteen years of war cost an estimated £4,500,000, and saddled the government with a debt of nearly £200,000. Further spending would have resulted in higher taxation, forced loans and onerous financial expedients that would have dented further Elizabeth's popularity and exacerbated social tensions. The 1590s were years of economic recession, bad harvests, and demographic reverses; and consequently many of Elizabeth's subjects found the strain of billeting and provisioning soldiers intolerable. It is questionable whether they would have countenanced higher taxes – in any event Elizabeth would not take the risk.

From the mid-1580s onwards a new breed of courtier began to frequent the royal palaces and attract the queen's favour. They were handsome swash-buckling types, men of action who could also charm the queen with their wit, poetry and courtly manners. In trying to catch her attention, the rivalry between them was intense and they tried to outdo each other in producing extravagant and inventive panegyric of the queen. Yet, despite their sycophantic words, these courtiers tended in practice to grow restless under her control. For many she was old enough to be their mother, or even grandmother, and they secretly mocked her and covertly challenged her authority by engaging in illicit sexual relations with her maids of honour. Walter Ralegh who became captain of her guard in 1587 was typical of these younger men. A soldier, adventurer, man of letters, and fine poet, he was a royal favourite until 1592 when his secret marriage to Elizabeth Throckmorton, a gentlewoman of the privy chamber, was revealed. Because he had previously denied the marriage, even after his wife's pregnancy, the queen briefly imprisoned him in the Tower and banished him from court indefinitely. Although he was not deprived of his various offices, he stayed away for five years.

This portrait of Sir Christopher Hatton, who was a firm favourite of Elizabeth, was painted two years before his death in 1591. Attached to the chain around his neck is a cameo of the queen which Hatton holds in his hand to display his devotion to her.
National Portrait Gallery

Ralegh's disgrace left his rival Robert Devereux 2nd earl of Essex as the unchallenged court favourite. Initially owing his place at court to his stepfather, Robert Dudley, earl of Leicester, Essex soon won royal approval. It should not be thought that Elizabeth was in love with him, but she certainly enjoyed his company, admired his looks, and felt deep affection for him as Leicester's heir. Yet Essex's relationship with the queen was always stormy. He was unbearably jealous of all rivals for the queen's favour, sulking or storming off when she showed attention to another. Frustrated by what he saw as her 'womanish' approach to military affairs and the cloying atmosphere of the court, he would set off for adventure abroad against her express wishes or retreat to the country in a mood of melancholy. For her part Elizabeth was roused to fury by his disobedience, self-promotion, and over-bearing arrogance. His alleged womanising also angered her. She was annoyed to hear of his secret marriage in 1590, but outraged to learn in 1595 that her maid of honour, Elizabeth Southwell, had borne him an illegitimate child four years earlier. Not only had Essex concealed his guilt from her all this time but he had also allowed another man to take the blame and be punished for the offence. Elizabeth, however, forgave Essex his philandering and tantrums in the hope that with time he would mature and control his behaviour.

Leicester died in September 1588 and his death affected Elizabeth badly; in her grief she secluded herself from her councillors, and for months afterwards she looked 'much aged and spent'. Till the end of her life, she kept his last note to her in a cabinet near her bed. Soon afterwards most of Elizabeth's other councillors who had dominated government since her accession followed him to the grave: Sir Walter Mildmay in 1589, Walsingham in 1590, and Sir Christopher Hatton (Elizabeth's one-time dancing partner who rose to become lord chancellor) in 1591. In 1596 she lost Hunsdon and Knollys; in 1597 Lord Cobham who was lord chamberlain and lord lieutenant of the Cinque Ports. Burghley survived them all, but was frequently incapacitated with gout, the stone and arthritis. He longed to retire but Elizabeth would not let him go. He eventually died in August 1598.

The gaps in the household and the council caused by these deaths were normally filled with the relatives of past or existing royal servants. The most important promotion of the 1590s was that of Burghley's younger son, Robert Cecil, who was made a councillor in 1591 and appointed secretary in 1596. Although unprepossessing in appearance – his short stature and hunchback earned him the nickname of 'pygmy' or 'elf'– he was shrewd, circumspect and intelligent. Elizabeth therefore elevated him over the head of Essex, who did not join the council until 1593 and had coveted the office of secretary for himself.

For a time, Essex maintained a cordial relationship with the Cecils, but by the end of 1596 their relations worsened. They disagreed over policy, with

Essex speaking out for an extension of the war against Spain while Robert Cecil favoured retrenchment and peace; in addition they competed over patronage as each tried to secure offices and grants for his clients. In these struggles Essex lost out, as Cecil won the argument over foreign policy and obtained the most prestigious posts for his friends. Essex, however, did not take defeat lightly and became increasingly antagonistic towards his rival: anyone who was a friend of Cecil's, he claimed, was his own enemy. As a result the court descended into a bitter factionalism. Although Essex's outlook and character were largely responsible for creating these political tensions, Elizabeth was not entirely blameless. She limited the rewards to be distributed for royal service, thereby intensifying the competition for patronage. Then she awarded Robert Cecil and his friends the bulk of offices vacated by death, and thus alienated Essex who sought them for his own followers. Finally she allowed Essex to treat her with a disrespect that weakened her authority and set him no boundaries.

At last in July 1598 Essex went too far and quarrelled irrevocably with Elizabeth. In the midst of an argument in council, he turned his back on her, a serious insult to any sovereign. 'She waxing impatient gave him a cuff on the ear, and bade him be gone with a vengeance'. Completely out of control, Essex laid his hand upon his sword and had to be restrained by another councillor present. Although a reconciliation of sorts took place some months later, it was only superficial and most of Essex's political credibility had been lost. Desperate to recover royal favour, he asked to be appointed lord lieutenant in Ireland. Elizabeth agreed and sent him off with a huge army of over 17,000 men to destroy the power of Hugh O'Neill, the rebellious Irish chieftain, who had just recently won a notable victory over English forces at Yellow Ford near Armagh.

HIC TVVS ILLE COMES GENEROSA ESSEXIA NOSTRIS
QVEM QVAM GAVDEMVS REBVS ADESSE DVCEM.

Essex achieved nothing in Ireland; he failed to engage O'Neill in battle and instead negotiated a truce with him. Elizabeth was dismayed at the waste of money, horrified at Essex's failure to obey orders, and even began to question his loyalty. Her disquiet grew, when on 28 September 1599 he returned to court against her explicit instructions. Unannounced he rushed into her bedchamber where he found her in a state of disarray, 'newly up, her hair about her face'. Although Elizabeth listened calmly to his speech of explanation, she had him confined to his chamber by nightfall and a few days afterwards he was placed in the custody of Lord Keeper Thomas Egerton. Elizabeth wanted him punished for his disobedience, but she bided her time until it seemed safe to bring him to trial, for she had to ensure that his following of hardened soldiers and young aristocrats did not stir up trouble.

In June 1600 Essex was put on trial and found guilty of 'great and high contempts'. Suspended from all his offices, except that of master of the horse, he was publicly humiliated and left without any political prospects. When in October 1600 Elizabeth refused to renew his lucrative monopoly on the customs duties of imported sweet wines, his debtors began closing in and he teetered on the brink of bankruptcy. As Sir John Harington, one of his supporters, wrote, he 'shifteth from sorrow and repentance to rage and rebellion so suddenly'. Listening to the advice of his wilder followers, Essex decided to mount a coup, and on Sunday 8 February 1601 he marched with about two hundred armed men through the streets of London, but contrary to his expectations none of the citizens joined him and the 'rebellion' fizzled out. Throughout the crisis, Elizabeth remained calm and did not hesitate to order his execution, although his betrayal and death clearly grieved her. Five rebels were executed with him, but the other leading participants, including the earl of Southampton, were reprieved.

At one level Essex's rebellion was hardly serious. Many of the earl's followers had deserted him well before he took to the streets, and the numbers involved in the conspiracy were small. Londoners remained loyal to the queen, despite the earl's popularity as a military hero. Nonetheless the rebels were representative of a wider group of soldiers, gentlemen and aristocrats who were disaffected and disillusioned with Elizabeth's rule. Furthermore, the earl's execution was unpopular and brought her reproach during her lifetime and beyond.

After the death of Essex, Elizabeth fell into a melancholy state. Her spirits were lifted somewhat by the news of the victory of Lord Mountjoy, her new lord lieutenant, over O'Neill's forces and the collapse of the rebellion in Ireland. Otherwise she had little cause for contentment during her final years. Her last parliament (1601) proved fractious with its members complaining about financial

SERO, SED SERIO

Robert Cecil, the younger son of Burghley, followed his father into political life. In 1591 at the age of twenty-eight he was sworn onto the privy council, to be its youngest ever member, and five years later he was appointed principal secretary.
National Portrait Gallery

burdens and governmental abuses. Although her health was generally good and she continued to ride and hunt, her advancing age could not be disguised. One foreign visitor noticed her 'wrinkled' face and 'her lips narrow and her teeth black'; although another one commented that 'even in old age she did not look ugly', he nonetheless added the words 'when seen from afar'. It was said that Elizabeth banished mirrors from her privy chamber. She certainly no longer participated in the vigorous dancing at court and had to be satisfied with watching younger people take to the floor. Moreover, she could no longer write in the elegant hand of her youth because of the gout that afflicted her fingers.

Despite her declining years, Elizabeth refused to name a successor. Few doubted, though, that she favoured the right of James VI of Scotland, as she had his mother before. She put considerable difficulties in the way of his main rivals, but anyone who openly advanced his claim was punished severely. As a result, Sir Robert Cecil, along with others, decided to correspond secretly with James and make covert plans to facilitate a smooth transfer of power.

In February 1603 in her seventieth year Elizabeth mourned the death of her friend and cousin, Katherine Carey countess of Nottingham. Soon afterwards, in March, she fell into 'a melancholy passion' and was unable to sleep; a little later she had problems with her throat and lost the power of speech, perhaps because of some streptococci infection or as the result of a stroke. At about 3 a.m. on 24 March she died with Archbishop Whitgift by her side. It was said that on her deathbed she indicated her wish for James to succeed, but this story was probably circulated in order to bolster his claim to the throne. Robert Carey galloped off to Scotland to be the first with the news, while the council and several nobles proclaimed James king of England. According to a London citizen, the proclamation was heard 'with great expectation and silent joy', and in the evening bonfires were lit and church bells rung to celebrate his accession.

The funeral of Elizabeth, which took place on 28 April 1603, provided the opportunity for English men and women to give vent to grief at their late queen's death. The size of the crowd watching the funeral procession is not recorded, but John Stow who attended the event described the onlookers' reactions to the sight of the painted effigy of the queen on top of the coffin: when the mourners, he wrote 'beheld her statue lying upon the coffin, there was such a general sighing, groaning and weeping as the like hath not been seen or known in the memory of man, neither doth any history mention any people, time or state to make like lamentation for the death of their sovereign.' Despite these open expressions of grief, most of the populace were nonetheless greatly relieved that their new monarch had succeeded to the throne without any challenge or disturbance. At the same time, many of James I's new subjects greeted his accession with an anticipation of better days to come. Political stability seemed assured with the presence on the throne of an adult king, who had live sons, and more than twenty years of experience in governing a realm. Protestants, moreover, were hopeful that James would permit the reforms in the English Church which Elizabeth had rejected, while Catholics fully expected him

When the mourners ... 'beheld her statue lying upon the coffin, there was such a general sighing, groaning and weeping as the like hath not been seen or known in the memory of man.'

to introduce a measure of religious toleration. It did not take long, however, for these expectations to be dashed, and by 1620 many at court and in the country were looking back with nostalgia to the reign of Good Queen Bess.

Today, the reputation of Elizabeth is mixed. Judging from opinion polls devised at the time of the new millennium, Elizabeth is both the best known and most respected of English monarchs. From anecdotal evidence it seems that much of her claim to fame amongst the general population today arises from her successful exercise of power in a man's world; people I meet are always referring to the strength of her leadership, her clever creation of an iconic image, and her magnetic personality. For them she seems to be the originator of 'power-dressing', 'spin-doctoring' and 'human resource management', a view promoted by the queen's portrayal in film and popular writing. Many, too, admire her personal bravery and intellectual capacity. Professional historians, however, are far more critical about Elizabeth's personal qualities and sceptical about her personal achievements. Many condemn her for vanity, capriciousness, indecisiveness, and a tendency to bully; they also tend to focus on the contemporary criticisms levelled against her rather than the plaudits and praise. Furthermore, it is becoming increasingly fashionable to marginalise the queen in accounts of her reign and instead to give credit to William Cecil for its most significant outcomes such as the Elizabethan Church settlement.

From this short biography it should be evident that I do not share this negative view of the queen; nor do I see her on the periphery of decision-making. Of course she had her character flaws and inevitably she made mistakes, but she was a charismatic and hands-on ruler, who proved a steady pair of hands during a period of political and religious ferment and helped save England from the religious civil wars that plagued her neighbours.

Chronology

1559	Coronation of Elizabeth (15 Jan); peace treaty is signed with France (April); Acts of Supremacy and Uniformity (April); death of Henry II of France and accession of Mary Stewart's husband, Francis II (July)
1560	Military intervention in Scotland ends with treaty of Edinburgh (July); death of wife of Robert Dudley (Sept); death of Francis II of France (Dec)
1561	Swedish marriage suit; Katherine Grey is sent to Tower (Aug) where she delivers her first son (Sept)
1562	English intervention in French civil war; Dudley and the duke of Norfolk are appointed to the privy council (Oct); Elizabeth is taken seriously ill with smallpox (Oct)
1563	39 Articles of Faith approved in convocation; English withdrawal from Le Havre (July)
1564	Robert Dudley is created earl of Leicester; Elizabeth clamps down on nonconformity in the Church
1565	Marriage of Mary Stewart to Henry Lord Darnley (July); arrival of Austrian envoy to negotiate a marriage between Elizabeth and Archduke Charles; Mary Grey punished for secret marriage
1566	Birth of James, son of Mary Stewart (June)
1567	Murder of Darnley (Feb); deposition of Mary Stewart as queen of Scotland (July)
1568	Death of Lady Katherine Grey (Jan); Mary's flight to England (May); trial of Mary at York (Sept)
1569	Norfolk's plan to marry Mary; Northern Rebellion (Nov)
1570	Papal bull of excommunication (Feb)
1571	Ridolfi Plot; William Cecil is created Lord Burghley
1572	Revolt in the Netherlands led by William of Orange
1572	Execution of Norfolk (June); St Bartholomew's massacre of Protestants in France (Aug)
1573	Sir Frances Walsingham is appointed principal secretary
1576	Elizabeth's order to suppress 'prophesyings'
1577	Elizabeth's suspension of Archbishop Edmund Grindal of Canterbury
1578	Opening of marriage negotiations with Francis duke of Anjou
1579	Anjou's arrival in England to court the queen (Aug); council debates the marriage (Oct)
1580	Arrival of first Jesuits

1581	Elizabeth subsidises Anjou's military campaign against Spain in the Netherlands; Anjou's second visit to England (Nov)
1583	Death of Archbishop Grindal (July) and elevation of John Whitgift to Canterbury; Throckmorton Plot (Oct)
1584	Death of Anjou (June); assassination of William of Orange (July); Bond of Association
1585	Drake sent to raid the West Indies; army ordered to the Netherlands under Leicester
1586	Babington plot to assassinate Elizabeth (July); trial and conviction of Mary (Oct)
1587	Elizabeth signs Mary's death warrant (1 Feb); Mary's execution (8 Feb)
1588	Defeat of the Spanish Armada (July); death of Robert Dudley, earl of Leicester (Sept)
1590	Death of Sir Francis Walsingham (Apr)
1591	Death of Sir Christopher Hatton (Nov)
1594	Beginning of a series of bad harvests
1595	Hugh O'Neill's rebellion in Ireland
1596	Essex's success at Cadiz; appointment of Robert Cecil as principal secretary
1598	Elizabeth's quarrel with Essex (July); death of William Cecil (Aug)
1599	Essex's unsuccessful campaign in Ireland; his arrest after returning without Elizabeth's consent
1600	Trial of Essex (June)
1601	Essex Revolt (Feb)
1603	Submission of O'Neill; death of Elizabeth I (24 Mar) and funeral (28 Apr); accession of James I

Further reading

Elizabeth's writings
Marcus, Leah S., Mueller, Janel and Rose, Mary Beth (eds.). *Elizabeth I: Collected Works* (University of Chicago Press, Chicago, 2000)

Biographies
Bassnet, Susan, *Elizabeth I: A Feminist Perspective* (London, 1988)

Neale, John, *Queen Elizabeth* (Jonathan Cape, London, 1934)

Somerset, Anne, *Elizabeth I* (Weidenfeld & Nicolson, London and New York, 1991)

Starkey, David, *Elizabeth I: Apprenticeship* (Ulverscroft, London, 2000)

Studies of the reign
Haigh, Christopher, *Elizabeth I* (Longman, Harlow, 1988 2nd edit 1998)

Jones, Norman, *The Birth of the Elizabethan Age England in the 1560s* (Blackwell, Oxford, 1993)

Levin Carole, *The Reign of Elizabeth I* (Palgrave, Basingstoke, 2002)

Sixteenth-century background
Brigden, Susan, *New Worlds, Lost Worlds: The Rule of the Tudors 1485-1603* (Penguin, London, 2001)
Collinson, Patrick, *The Sixteenth Century – 1485-1603* (Oxford University Press, Oxford, 2001)

Doran, Susan and Durston, Christopher, *Princes, Pastors and People: The Church and Religion in England 1500-1700* (Routledge, London, 2nd edition, 2002)

Specialist studies
Arnold, Janet, *Queen Elizabeth's Wardrobe Unlock'd* (W.S. Maney and Sons Ltd, Leeds, 1988)

Doran, Susan, *Monarchy and Matrimony: The Courtships of Elizabeth I* (Routledge, London, 1996)

Doran, Susan and Freeman, Thomas S., (eds.), *The Myth of Elizabeth I* (Palgrave, Basingstoke, 2003)

Hackett, Helen, *Virgin Mother, Maiden Queen: Elizabeth I and the Cult of the Virgin Mary* (Macmillan, Basingstoke, 1994)

Neale, John E., *Elizabeth I and her Parliaments*, 2 vols (Jonathan Cape, London, 1953 and 1957, repr. 1971)

Strong, Roy, *Gloriana: The Portraits of Queen Elizabeth I* (Thames and Hudson, London, 1987)

Strong, Roy, *The Cult of Elizabeth: Elizabethan Portraiture and Pageantry* (Thames and Hudson, London, 1977)

Index

Opt. Max. Ser.^tem V.^tram in fo[...]
fidei Christianæ hostes re[...]
Ser.^tis Victoria & successu
diutissime florentem seruet
Westmonasterij die Men[...]
LXXI Regni nri decimo